Leadership in Diversity and Inclusion

Ultimate Management Guide to Challenging Bias, Creating Organizational Change, and Building an Effective Diversity and Inclusion Strategy

Add cultural awareness

Eleanor Bowes

Table of Contents

Introduction

The ability to listen to others' points of view is a critical skill for any successful leader. Whether you're the CEO of a Fortune 500 company or a teacher in an elementary school classroom, if you surround yourself with "yes men" and only listen to the voices of people who share your experiences, you're going to miss out on a wealth of information that could help you become a better boss, administrator, or collaborator. With a greater focus on diversity, you might learn how to market a product to different demographics, become more adept at connecting with people from different backgrounds, and strengthen your interpersonal skills. The more diverse sources of information and opinions you have access to, the more informed you'll be when you need to make important decisions as a leader.

Additionally, the diversity of workplaces and other organizations only increases each year. Diversity and inclusion aren't just about hiring to fill a quota. They're also about creating a culture that values each member of your team equally, where no voices are drowned out because of someone's race, gender, religion, culture, language, sexual orientation, or disabilities. Nuance is required when trying to turn a rapidly-diversifying workforce into a fully functioning team, all in a way that minimizes conflicts and encourages collaboration.

1

Recently, there has been a movement to replace outdated methods of communication in the workplace and root out inappropriate behavior. When team members feel uncomfortable because of the words or actions of their peers or superiors, they're less likely to share their ideas or feel like a real part of the team. Harmful interactions can interfere with building a welcoming culture and drive people away. Once identified, these negative interactions can then be replaced by more collaborative, constructive ones that account for and respect peoples' differences, so that no member of your team feels like they are an outsider or less valued than their coworkers. A great company or group culture can serve as the foundation from which significant positive changes can grow.

Diversity and inclusion efforts are key contributing factors for success in companies and organizations of all sizes. Diversity has become an important buzzword in leadership lately, yet some still treat it as an obligation. In reality, it is an opportunity to give a platform to a wide demographic of different voices. The more diverse and inclusive your organization is, the more perspectives get to have a seat at the table, and the more likely you are to hear new, exciting ideas that challenge the status quo. The ideal is not just to become someone who *practices* diversity and inclusion, but to become a *champion* for inclusivity within your organization. As you begin to understand just how useful these two factors can be and why they're so important to creating a healthy, positive culture, you will become a more effective and reliable leader for your whole team, and the hidden potential of your business or organization will be revealed.

In *Leadership in Diversity and Inclusion*, you'll learn how you can become a champion of diversity and inclusivity. You'll read about real examples of the positive effects diversity strategies can have on success. You'll also learn about some of the difficulties that come with trying to create an inclusive environment and how you can avoid common missteps. Each of these skills will help you become a more capable leader in your field, assisting you in making the workplace or organization as inclusive as possible and helping you attract the right kind of talent for your business or organization.

Interpersonal conflicts spurred by bigotry and exclusion, whether intentional or accidental, can harm the health of your organization. Diversity and inclusion efforts are paramount to success in companies and classrooms alike. By developing a positive attitude toward diversity and inclusion, and taking proactive steps to make sure everyone has a voice—not just in spite of their differences but because of them—you'll take a leading role in creating a motivating and nurturing environment that ensures everyone is able to put their best foot forward.

Chapter 1: Diversity in North America

While diversity itself is nothing new, it has become a highly relevant concern for most modern-day organizations. This is in part because of shifting attitudes that have put a spotlight on difficulties with inclusion that have previously gone overlooked, but it can also be partially attributed to the increasing level of diversity that can be seen in workplaces, schools, and groups all across North America. Studies from organizations like the Pew Research Center, which studies demographic trends and social issues, found that "Americans are more racially and ethnically diverse than in the past," and projections suggest that "by 2055, the U.S. will not have a single racial or ethnic majority" (Cohn & Caumont, 2016, para. 2). Diversity has generally increased across U.S. history, and this trend has only become more significant as social movements bring advocacy for minority groups into the public spotlight.

The United States has long been referred to as a "melting pot" where many people of diverse backgrounds and cultures have contributed to an overarching national culture. However, even within the nation, there are many distinct cultural areas with different kinds of people. The lifestyle of someone living in the Northeast part of the country is likely going to differ significantly from that of someone living in the Midwest, and their beliefs and values may also differ accordingly. Even within a single company, there may be people of different races, religions, ages, genders, and sexualities, all of whom have equally diverse perspectives on a variety of issues. For this reason, some have chosen to refer to the United States as a "mosaic" rather than a melting pot, made up of an assortment of distinct yet interconnected groups coming together to create one whole picture. This model accounts for the fact that these personal and cultural differences can remain disparate, with everyone's beliefs being accounted for rather than assimilated into a singular culture, and still come together to yield a stronger result than if they had stayed separate. This is a foundational example of the importance and power of diversity.

Of course, this trend is equally present throughout the rest of North America. Countries like Canada and Mexico are also becoming more diverse, as are their workforces, living spaces, and organizations. For example, as of 2016 "more than one-fifth of Canadians are people of color," which is projected to rise to "about a third (31% to 36%) of the population" by 2036 following increasing immigration rates (Catalyst, 2020, para. 2-3). As diversity increases across the continent, workplace diversity is an especially important development, as employers and employees alike adjust to changes in the working environment.

Workforce Diversity Trends

Diversity has significantly skyrocketed in workforces across North America, to the point that most workplaces, large and small, are more culturally, racially, and ethnically diverse than ever before. While there are still some significant levels of racial disparity in the workplace, with about "78 percent" of the U.S. labor force being white as of 2018, this means members of racial minority groups made up the remaining 22%, and this number is only projected to grow in future years. Of these racial groups, black and Asian people "constituted an additional 13 percent and 6 percent, respectively." Additionally, "Seventeen percent of the labor force were people of Hispanic or Latino ethnicity," 89% of whom were white (Bureau of Labor Statistics, 2019, para. 6-7). Racial diversity is just one part of the puzzle, but it's a good indicator of the growing demand for accepting, inclusive policies that reduce the risk of racial discrimination in both the hiring process and everyday situations at the office.

Workplaces are also inclusive of a higher degree of differing genders and sexualities in the workforce than they were a decade ago. Though still somewhat underrepresented in high-paying jobs and upper-ladder roles compared to their male peers, according to the U.S. Department of Labor women make up "Almost 47 percent of U.S. workers," with "74.6 million women in the civilian labor force" (DeWolf, 2017, para. 2). There are many lesbian, gay, bisexual, and/or transgender (LGBT) individuals in the workforce as well, many of whom want to feel accepted and treated with respect by their managers and coworkers.

People belonging to one or more minority group are more likely to seek out employment somewhere they feel safe and welcome, which is part of the reason why a diverse workplace is so important for today's companies. If employees don't feel like they're being respected, if they face consistent harassment at their jobs, or if they are prevented from receiving promotions or raises due to their race, religion, gender, or sexual orientation, they may choose to take their talents elsewhere. To this end, many CEOs and bosses have made efforts to account for and accommodate this ever-expanding diverse workforce.

Trends in Accommodating Diversity

Company owners and administrators have long since felt the need to change and adapt to accommodate greater diversity. In 2020, the need to overhaul old rules and regulations and focus efforts on building the diversity of a company's workforce have been brought to center stage by protests and social movements taking place across the globe. As a result, many CEOs have taken steps to improve these regulations within their companies in a variety of ways.

Some of these trends take place on the hiring level. Building a diverse workforce means making a conscious effort to reach out and attract people of different backgrounds and demographics, as well as avoiding making hiring decisions based on biases and prejudices. Many companies are beginning to actively seek out employees of different races, religions, sexualities, and genders. They're also evaluating the demographics of their upper-level positions and restructuring them to make upward mobility possible for people who may have previously been overlooked. As more diverse voices join the conversations, hiring policies slowly and surely become more inclusive.

Other diversity accommodation trends take place within the company structure. These include attempts to root out and eliminate the underlying causes of hostile working environments, engage in team-building exercises that foster respect and connection within diverse groups, and implementing more inclusive policies with a strong impact on company culture. These kinds of regulatory changes have become commonplace in successful businesses throughout North America. We will discuss the benefits of utilizing inclusive strategies in more detail in Chapter 4; for now, it is important to note that typically the returns companies see when they focus on diversity and inclusion are well worth the time and effort they expend on implementing them.

Difficulties in Addressing Workplace Diversity

While there are laws prohibiting purposeful discrimination in the hiring process, personal biases, consciously or unconsciously, can still interfere in even the most well-intentioned efforts to practice inclusive leadership. There may be discriminatory practices at play that aren't readily apparent to you, but which may be all too obvious from the perspectives of your employees or group members who are most hurt by them. For example, different religious groups have different days of rest and requirements for prayer. Many Christians view Sunday as the day of rest and may attend church services in the mornings, while the Jewish faith recognizes Saturday as the day of rest. Despite this, many companies require their employees to come in on Saturdays and not Sundays. Accommodating some employees' religious practices and not others, even if it is simply because you didn't know about these differences, can create barriers that prevent the workplace from feeling truly inclusive.

Wage gaps and discrepancies in promotions can interfere with diversity initiatives as well. Recently, advocates have started bringing attention to the pay gap between men and women who work the same job. There is also the concept of the "glass ceiling," which refers to the lower likelihood for women and people in minority groups to be promoted to higher roles in the company. At a certain point, they hit this invisible ceiling, and are often passed over for men of similar or sometimes lesser skill and experience levels. The glass ceiling is especially insidious because most company and organization leaders don't recognize its presence and aren't consciously choosing not to promote women, and yet the trend persists across hundreds of industries. It is an important issue to tackle for any diversity and inclusion plan, as are the other systematic and individual-level issues that can be addressed and corrected with effective new policies.

It is important to consider diversity from all angles while creating inclusive policies. Gender, religion, sexual identity, culture, language, and disabilities are all axes of diversity that should be accounted for. While this book primarily deals with racial diversity and inclusion strategies, these other diversity trends will be periodically touched on as well. With a comprehensive inclusion strategy, these roadblocks to addressing diversity issues are removed, and real progress toward an equitable and welcoming workplace or organization can be made.

Chapter 2: The Growing Need for Companies to Adopt a Diversity and Inclusion Strategy

As demographics shift in workplaces, it is no longer enough to pay little to no attention to diversity within a company and assume all will be well. In this kind of environment, the previously mentioned uncommon biases can become more pronounced when left unchecked. Seemingly harmless policies can have severe negative impacts on the workplace culture and the experience of people in minority groups while working for the company. The best way to eliminate the risk of conscious or unconscious biases defining workplace culture is to get ahead of the curve. In other words, it is necessary to adopt and implement a diversity and inclusion strategy in all companies, before the situation becomes intolerable for employees.

The culture of any workplace or group will begin to define itself naturally over time. As group members become more comfortable with each other and get a sense of what is and isn't okay to say and do at work, this will become the norm. Company culture will exist whether or not you are there to guide its development. Of course, there are some cultures that are more productive and valuable than others. Cultures that promote inclusivity, positivity, responsibility, and diligence ensure everyone knows they're expected to perform their best and treat their coworkers with respect. However, if too many people spread negativity or unconscious biases go unchecked among employees for a long time, the culture can devolve into one that breeds resentment for spending time at work and negatively impacts everyone.

To start creating or correcting a workplace culture, consider the values you find to be most important. Maybe you want your team members to feel like they're family, but can they really come to rely on each other if some are uncomfortable due to tension and discrimination in the workplace? It's great to strive for productivity, but if some employees have a better chance of getting promoted than others simply because of their race or gender and not because of the quality of their work, then there is little reason for anyone else to work hard, since they know they'll always be looked over. Your company values cannot exist in a vacuum. They must be clearly reflected in your policies. If you want your team to work effectively, then you must lead the way. Start by recognizing instances of inequality that occur within the group, then begin the implementation of diversity and inclusion policies to counteract these inequalities.

Recognizing Inequality

Inequality is often perpetuated in the workplace or other organizations not because managers and CEOs are knowingly trying to be racist, sexist, ableist, homophobic, or practice other prejudices, but because inequality can so effectively fly under the rader for those who aren't directly impacted by it. Not every instance of racism is as cut-and-dry as setting aside a job application because the applicant's name "sounds nonwhite." Racism and other prejudices can pervade groups in far more subtle ways.

For example, many workplace dress codes are stricter for women than they are for men. Many offices require women to wear high-heels and skirts or dresses rather than pants, as these are seen as more formal clothing items, regardless of the discomfort this may cause women. There's also a social expectation for women to wear makeup to "look professional" when they come into the office, while men rarely if ever are expected to do the same. Worse, many company dress codes suggest these policies are only in place to ensure women don't "distract their coworkers," suggesting both that male coworkers cannot behave appropriately in the workplace and that women are at fault should inappropriate behavior occur. People of color also face greater levels of scrutinization from dress codes, as some outfits with cultural significance may be barred from the workplace. Even a policy requiring haircuts to look "professional" is operating under a certain definition of what the word professional entails, and this definition may leave no room for some people of color with naturally curly hair, locks, or extensions.

Some policies even target religious articles of clothing like yarmulkes or kippahs, turbans, and headscarves like hijabs, burkas, and niqabs, even while necklaces or pins with Christian crosses are allowed. It's important that any company dress code is fair for every employee, applying rules that account for everyone's differences even if professional attire is required. If your main concern is employee productivity, ask yourself what hurts productivity more: an employee wearing a hijab, which doesn't interfere with their work in any way, or an employee quitting because of restrictive, discriminatory policies.

Of course, subconscious and less recognizable forms of bias don't just stop at dress codes. Other examples include pay gaps between men and women, especially women of color; continual and unwelcome questions about "cultural differences" that become harassment; differences in providing feedback; and looking for commonalities during the hiring and interviewing process as a way to connect with candidates rather than embracing peoples' differences. These aren't quite as easy to identify and call out as many of the more blatant types of discrimination that can pervade a group, but they can cause similar amounts of harm. Developing inclusive policies that account for the diverse differences of everyone who might join your workforce alleviates these issues. Thinking more critically about company policies, even ones that have been in place for a long time, keeps you from unknowingly making mistakes that hurt you employees and ensures no one is made to feel uncomfortable, unrecognized, or targeted at work.

Reasons to Begin Implementing Diversity and Inclusion Policies

Diversity and inclusion policies have significant benefits that can really change how a group operates. These benefits aren't just for people of minority groups; they extend to everyone in the company. When everyone gets to work on an even playing field and collaborate together, everyone enjoys the positive results, in both quality of work and quality of life.

Attract More Talent

If you go the extra mile to make your company more welcoming for diverse groups of people, potential hires will take notice. Many people, especially those who have faced discrimination in the past, look for workplaces where they can feel comfortable and safe before accepting any job offer. If you don't have any efforts to promote diversity and inclusion in your company, people might worry about feeling ostracized, even if there's little or no actual discrimination at the company. When you make a name for yourself as a group that welcomes diversity, you'll attract plenty of talent you might have otherwise missed out on.

Improve Productivity and Output

Employees often work harder and care about the quality of their work more when they're personally invested in the company's success. If they feel they're being mistreated at work, they may care less about their output and feel less motivated overall. Low employee engagement can lead to poor quality of work, missed deadlines, and little quality control. Diversity and inclusion measures help employees feel more connected to their companies and inspired to put forth their best efforts. Notably, surveys of Canadian companies who have implemented diversity-focused policies cited "enhance employee engagement" as the most important reason for these policies to exist, coming in just ahead of "enhance ability to acquire new talent" and "brand the organization externally" (Garr, Shellenback, & Scales, 2014, p. 18). Engagement is as important to employees of these companies as it is to their managerial staff. When everyone is engaged, productivity and work quality soar, which is a huge benefit to any organization.

Embrace New Perspectives

Greater employee and management diversity brings new perspectives to conversations that would have otherwise been missing them. The more diverse your workforce, the more people you have contributing to the conversation, and the more unique ideas and problem-solving skills you have at your disposal. For example, if your company is trying to market your product to different demographics, you might have a hard time appealing to these groups if you never talk to anyone from them. You might also let an unconscious bias affect your work if there's no one to recognize it and call it out, which could harm your public perception and hurt your sales if offended customers refuse to engage with your company. With more diversity, you have a larger pool of experiences from which to pull new ideas and catch mistakes before they undergo public scrutiny.

Improve Company Decision-Making

Some company leaders try to do all the major decision-making on their own. They believe they know what's best for their companies, and they believe this "my way or the highway" style of leadership ensures everything follows their vision for their company. However, this is a dangerous and often ineffective way to lead, since a single person can only draw from their own experiences. If they lack knowledge in a given area, they might make the wrong decisions. Even leaders of nations have cabinets to direct them on matters they might not be experts on, so why shouldn't companies?

You can be a more effective leader by seeking out diverse perspectives and listening to others' input when you make decisions. While the choice of how to resolve a given issue is ultimately yours to make, getting input from others can reveal things you wouldn't otherwise have considered. In a study of both diverse and non-diverse teams run by the online decision-making platform Cloverpop, results revealed that "diverse teams have a 60 percent improvement in decision-making," with "gender-diverse teams [outperforming] individual decision makers 73 percent of the time, and teams diverse in geography, gender, and age [making] better business decisions than individuals 87 percent of the time" (Wong, 2020, para. 16). You might be missing out on significant advantages without diversity in your company.

Making the Workplace Inclusive, Not Just Diverse

Increasing diversity in the workplace is great, but it's only a starting step. It does very little to actually impact company culture if subtle methods of discrimination still persist. Bringing more staff from racialized groups into the company is just one part of the inclusivity puzzle, but if these new employees don't feel like they're being valued, or if the company culture still unfairly targets people of color, you haven't yet accomplished your goal. Consider the racial tensions and systemic racism that still plagues North America despite the rising diversity. The laws and public perceptions that create these systemic issues haven't changed much, so the experiences of minority groups have changed very little too. Diversity alone won't help your company achieve real, long-lasting positive change if you can't back the diversity up with inclusive policies. In other words, true inclusivity involves taking actions to make a diverse workforce feel like their contributions are valued and reduces the risk of hiring diversely just to fulfill a quota.

Prioritizing inclusion, not just diversity, is a key factor in ensuring your new policies are effective. To do so, you'll need to first understand the differences between diversity and inclusion, and recognize how anti-racist and anti-discriminatory policies do more to promote equality and equity in group environments than diversity efforts alone.

Chapter 3: The Difference Between Diversity and Inclusion

Diversity rates are increasing across North America, yet there's still an ever-growing need for policies in groups and workplaces that properly address this diversity. In the wake of recent social movements, many companies made an effort to employ a more diverse workforce. While these efforts were a good step forward, they often did little to address the systemic problems affecting people in minority groups in the workplace. Additionally, even though there is plenty of research serving as evidence of the benefits of greater diversity in the workplace, many of these companies didn't see the improvement they expected in productivity, company culture, or output. Why did this happen?

In short, these companies improved their diversity, but they failed to also improve their inclusivity. Without policies that promoted inclusivity, there were more nonwhite, female, LGBT, disabled, and religious minority employees, but these employees were still routinely being passed over in favor of straight, white, male, non-disabled, Christian employees. Their ideas were undervalued, even though many management teams didn't recognize the harmful practices they were perpetuating. Jokes at the expense of minority groups and other harmful language were still commonplace around the watercooler. Company policies existed that interfered with their ability to express themselves, such as restricting dress codes that unfairly targeted women or rules that interfered with certain religious practices, but these policies largely remained in place with brush-offs like "those are the rules, they've been that way forever." Even though the demographics of the workplace changed, the conditions for people in minority groups didn't improve because there was no effort made to actually include them.

Diversity and inclusion are frequently lumped together, and in some regards they are connected. However, they actually refer to quite different things. Diversity is more descriptive of the demographics of a group, while inclusion refers to how the group members feel and how different policies affect them. Describing a group as diverse "refers to political beliefs, race, culture, sexual orientation, religion, class, and/or gender identity differences. In the workplace, diversity means your staff consists of individuals who bring new perspectives and backgrounds to the table" (Wong, 2020, para. 6). A diverse staff is important, as without it you might only hear ideas from a single demographic, or only consider your own ideas when making decisions. Simply having a more diverse workforce can go a long way toward showing people of different backgrounds that you're interested in working with them, as well as normalizing more inclusive efforts, but it doesn't result in inclusion on its own.

Inclusion, on the other hand, is the culmination of actual policies and a purposefully crafted company culture. It refers to the impact of these policies on each of the group's members. Maintaining an inclusive environment "means that everyone in the diverse mix feels involved, valued, respected, treated fairly, and embedded in your culture. Empowering all employees and recognizing their special talents is part of creating an inclusive company" (Wong, 2020, para. 7). Organizations that value inclusivity build upon a foundation of diversity to create a positive environment for all members.

Inclusion and diversity must coexist to be entirely successful. As a good leader, you cannot and should not have one without the other. Diversity without inclusion does nothing to help your employees feel safe and respected in your organization. People who are part of minority groups may feel like they're only there to fill a quota, and that they have become the "token representative" for their race, religion, gender, class, or sexuality. They may very quickly become fed up with being talked over and excluded and decide to leave the group on their own, or they may attempt to contribute but always feel like they're on the outer edges of the team. On the other hand, inclusion without diversity doesn't help anyone either. It might look nice to outside observers if you have inclusive policies, but if no one is actually benefiting from them because there's no diversity in the group, these policies come off more as paying lip service to inclusion than actually practicing it.

When both policies are present, they reinforce each other and have a stronger cumulative effect. A more diverse company lends itself well to the creation of more inclusive policies, as people from all demographics weigh in on possible barriers to inclusion. As a leader, you can work alongside each of your group's members, listening to their concerns and asking for their input about solutions that they believe would resolve the issues they experience. Additionally, if your organization becomes notable for its inclusivity, you're more likely to attract a diverse pool of job or membership candidates who are eager and excited to join your team.

In order to start implementing inclusive guidelines, you must first have a good understanding of exactly what inclusion means and how it elevates diversity efforts to their natural next step.

Understanding Inclusion

At its most basic level, inclusion is about ensuring every group member enjoys the same rights and privileges as their peers. For a company to call itself inclusive, there must be no policies that unfairly impact certain groups, and no biases that pervade the company culture and discourage certain people from taking part in activities or speaking up so their input can be heard. Inclusive guidelines protect the basic rights of employees and team members. They facilitate positive interactions between group members and ensure everyone is acting respectfully at all times. When everyone is included, everyone can meaningfully participate in their work and the projects they're expected to handle.

To be clear, being inclusive does not mean giving people from minority groups special rights or privileges over others. If two of a company's employees of different races break the same rule, one should not receive a harsher punishment than the other, regardless of who it goes to. This just perpetuates inequality, and it can breed resentment within the rest of the workforce. Additionally, few, if any people who want to see inclusive policies implemented are asking for preferential treatment. Instead, they just want to know they'll be treated the same way as anyone else so they can feel like they're a member of the team.

Inclusion efforts should include policies that protect group members' rights, as well as social norms and common practices that reinforce these policies. Social norms can be just as, if not more, important than the rules themselves, as these dictate how everyone treats each other. Rules against discrimination can only go so far on their own. You can restrict discriminatory language, but this doesn't mean that everyone will suddenly feel more accepting toward coworkers in minority groups. They may still be excluded from certain projects or get-togethers outside the workplace. By shaping the group's social norms, setting a positive example and expecting everyone to follow your lead, you tell your team members what is and isn't acceptable behavior. If you set a precedent of inviting everyone along to fun company activities, facilitating interactions and rewarding good teamwork, the other members of the group will see your actions and follow them. Eventually, once everyone knows what acceptable behavior looks like, your team may even start policing instances of unacceptable behavior themselves, confronting coworkers who use derogatory terms or reporting these incidents to you rather than laughing along with a crude joke.

Be careful not to confuse inclusion with tolerance. While tolerance isn't necessarily a bad thing, it has fairly different implications. If you tolerate a behavior, you allow it to continue without supporting or rejecting it. You take a permissive role rather than an encouraging one. Tolerating someone's differences might look like saying it's okay for a Muslim employee to pray, but also telling them you don't want to hear about it. You might tolerate one of your employees being in a gay relationship but tell them you don't want to see them hug or kiss their spouse or partner, even though you'd have no problem seeing two people in a straight relationship do the same. Tolerance doesn't require you to choose a side. Inclusion, on the other hand, means you need to actively advocate for peoples' differences. This doesn't mean you must constantly bring them up in conversation, but try to be open to the idea of seeing and understanding what makes everyone unique. Don't just tolerate their differences; accept and celebrate them, and use them as a way to increase collaboration within the team based on everyone's strengths and weaknesses. Over time, this will do far more to strengthen bonds between team members than "don't ask, don't tell" style policies that tend to brush these differences under the rug.

What an Inclusive Organization Looks Like

Not everything can be achieved through policies and rules. Some inclusivity efforts must be presented through more natural methods, becoming baked in to the core of the company culture. Once you've started laying out inclusive policies and expecting your team members to follow them, the social norms of your group will shift, and you'll start creating a genuinely inclusive organization.

First and foremost, inclusive organizations have actively inclusive leaders. Leading through example is one of the best ways to get everyone to care about and celebrate diversity. If you want others to follow your rules, you need to follow them yourself, or people will assume it's okay to break them and get away with it. Keep a careful eye on your own behaviors, and periodically evaluate your decisions to check for any biases. Go into discussions with an open mind, ready to hear a new perspective. Be open to change and corrections when you've overstepped or misunderstood, and try not to get defensive when someone points these missteps out. Instead, learn from the experience, assure the other person their concerns are being listened to, and take immediate steps to correct the issue before it happens again depending on the problem.

Feedback is an incredibly useful tool for you as a leader. The leaders of inclusive organizations are always looking for feedback from their employees about their policies and their demeanor, as well as things like how the company is run and what kind of improvements could be made. Ask for periodic, routine feedback, and invite everyone to join the conversation. Additionally, be open to different methods for collecting feedback. Many leaders are set in their ways and use only traditional methods of gathering employees' opinions. While it's nice to be able to sit down with people one-on-one and discuss any issues they might be having in a monthly review, these reviews can also put people on the spot and make them feel like they're the ones being evaluated. They may be more hesitant to speak up about issues, especially if they fear retaliation in the form of losing their job, getting a pay cut, or missing out on a promotion. These fears can be made worse if you look for feedback in a group setting, as some people may not want to discuss problems they've been facing in front of the very people who have been causing these issues. Anonymous forms of feedback can work wonders for getting peoples' genuine opinions, as no one is worried they'll be singled out for what they say. Let people write comments and suggestions on pieces of paper and drop them in a suggestion box for your review, or have them fill out online surveys where they don't need to give their names. The less employees worry about their comments being traced back to them, the more honest they can be.

Using inclusive language is another way to become a more inclusive organization. Even though it seems like such a small thing, language can make a big difference in how we interact with others. As an example, you might replace a phrase like "Hey guys" in your emails with one that includes everyone like "Hello all!" or something bright to start the message such as "Hope everyone's having a great day!" Use gender-neutral pronouns like 'they' rather than "he/she" where applicable. You might even consider giving your group members a fun name based on the name of your organization, which helps everyone feel like a team. The ways you choose to describe things can impact peoples' perception of them in surprisingly powerful ways. A deadline feels more pressing than a due date. A punishment sounds harsher than a consequence. Small changes like these can help people reframe negative interactions in a more positive, constructive light. The same is true with using inclusive language to everyone's benefit. Other ways to use inclusive language include using peoples' correct pronouns when you address them, emphasizing humanity (for example, saying "gay people" instead of "gays" or "people with disabilities" rather than "the handicapped"), eliminating phrases based on harmful stereotypes from your vocabulary (for example, phrases alluding to Jewish people being stingy), and using more general terms like "happy holidays" when not talking about a specific religion. Remember that you will have many people under your command who live different lifestyles, and you should try to account for these in your language whenever possible. These are small yet highly impactful gestures that your team members will notice and appreciate.

Inclusive groups typically have diversity not just within the lower levels of the workforce, but in the upper levels too. Hiring and management are two especially key areas to focus on. Diverse hiring managers are more likely to attract and approve diverse candidates, and they'll have less difficulty disregarding internalized biases in the hiring process. They're also more likely to notice if a certain demographic is underrepresented in your organization, and they can work to correct the issue. Diversity in management is equally important, as people generally feel more comfortable raising their concerns to human resources (HR) and their bosses when they know they have someone on their side. This is especially important for sensitive issues that may be mishandled or be embarrassing to discuss with people outside of a certain group. For example, a woman facing sexual harassment by one of her coworkers might be more likely to report the incident to another woman, as she'll likely feel her concerns are taken more seriously and that she can trust a fellow woman to understand why the harassment is an issue. For cultural and religious issues, employees facing problems won't need to spend as much time explaining why something is a problem if they can talk to someone who shares their culture or religion. In general, people in management, disciplinary, and hiring positions should be open-minded, diversity positive, and sympathetic, but ensuring these positions are filled out with diverse workers is a great way to go the extra mile for your teammates.

The hallmark of an inclusive organization is successful collaboration between employees of different backgrounds and demographics. Your team should work as one cohesive unit without significant tensions between members. Of course, this doesn't mean everyone needs to be best friends and spend time together outside of work. There's little you can do authentically to forge these kinds of connections as a leader, and some people just aren't going to become friends no matter what you do. However, they should still be able to discuss and complete projects with each other when necessary. If there is a problem between two or more people that's big enough that it's disrupting workflow, speak to all parties and attempt to get to the root of the conflict so you can decide on the best solution. Sometimes you'll need to make tough decisions and you may even need to let an employee go if their behavior is especially egregious, but this is better than the alternative of letting people in the company resent each other or forcing someone to work with a coworker who doesn't show them respect. In a truly inclusive company, everyone receives the respect they deserve, so good conflict resolution skills are especially useful here.

Finally, many inclusive organizations extend their policies and company climate past the basics needed for diversity and inclusivity. Many companies, now more than ever, are adopting antiracist policies. These policies take a more active role in rooting out sources of prejudice, creating a no-tolerance environment for discriminatory actions.

Embracing Antiracism

Many activists for the rights of people of color have pointed out that it is no longer enough to simply not be racist. You can refrain from implementing racist policies and not use discrimination in the workplace, but if you never call out racism when you see it, and you never work with the specific goal of eliminating prejudice within the company, you are still permitting racist actions to occur. As a leader, it is especially important for you to take this extra step and ensure there are no interactions occurring between your team members that are motivated by racism, so everyone can feel like they're equally respected. In addition to diversity and inclusion strategies, you can extend these efforts into a more active form of dealing with the biases and prejudices of others known as antiracism.

Antiracism works to challenge long-held beliefs and systems of power that are all too often taken for granted. Taking an anti-racist approach to leadership involves adopting "an action-oriented strategy for institutional and systemic change that has at its core the interrogation of privilege, power disparities, and other forms of inequity within the organization" (Hiranandani, 2012, para. 1). It is a more effective method for combating racism in the workplace than the well-intentioned diversity measures that often fall flat on their own. Antiracism challenges leaders and their team members to consider the larger power dynamics at play that can influence workplace culture, and to purposefully engage themselves in promoting equality and equity.

Antiracism in action can take a policy or social norm approach, just like making a group more inclusive. As an example of where policy is most effective, consider that in both the U.S. and Canada there's a significant pay gap between the earnings of black employees, especially black women, and the salaries their white male counterparts are paid. There are many justifications for this difference in pay, but they are flimsy at best and based on actively harmful stereotypes at worst. Continuing to perpetuate this pay gap, even though it may not be unique to your company, is still perpetuating a system steeped in racist policies and actions. An anti-racist approach to solving this issue doesn't just stop at giving people equal pay for equal work; it also challenges the inherent beliefs behind the idea that it's okay to pay black women less for their work. It questions how those beliefs found their way into your company, and begs the question of what you will do from preventing similar situations from occurring in the future. An antiracist view of wage gaps showcases how they're part of a distressingly common systemic issue rather than the result of a single person's actions. You may also consider how this wage gap can perpetuate other forms of inequality, such as black mothers being more likely to live below the poverty line and face food insecurity as compared to white mothers. Now that you understand the issue as systemic, not just a one-off mistake, you can keep an eye out for similarly subtle forms of racism within the company and take an active role in putting a stop to them.

Antiracism can also come in the form of conversations and corrections that hold up the values of the policies you've implemented. Consider the following situation: you're having a casual conversation with one of your team members when they make a joke that stems from prejudices. You have two options in this situation. First, you could brush it aside, decide you don't want to police anyone's language, and move on. This might be the more comfortable solution for both of you, but your ability to be passive in this situation comes from a place of privilege. The joke didn't directly target or hurt you, so it's "not a big deal" and it can be easily ignored. This is how easy it is to let racist actions and language persist within a group. Your other option is to halt the conversation, draw attention to what your team member said while pointing out why it's hurtful, and ask them not to say it again. You might feel like a

"Debbie downer" if you're not used to making these kinds of interruptions, but as a leader in diversity and inclusion, it's your job to speak up when you hear someone perpetuating prejudices. This is the better option for your organization in the long run, as it tells your team that their language matters and it can be hurtful. It teaches them what you consider to be unacceptable in creating a welcoming environment where everyone can feel safe.

Antiracism is the mark of a true leader in diversity and inclusion, as it represents a zero-tolerance policy for racist words and actions that could hurt team members. It may be true that you yourself are not racist, but this isn't enough to create an environment free of racism, nor is it enough if you don't recognize how your actions are influenced by subtle, pervasive forms of prejudice. Even if you don't mean to perpetuate racism, you may still say or do the wrong thing and cause harm to others. Antiracism is the most effective step in eliminating negative attitudes and biases about specific racial, cultural, and ethnic groups. It is about recognizing the presence of systemic racism, which often goes ignored or overlooked, and the ways it offers an advantage to some while disadvantaging others. By practicing antiracism, you will learn to look at your policies and actions with a self-critical eye and feel more comfortable calling out things that perpetuate discrimination, which goes a long way toward establishing a truly inclusive environment.

Chapter 4: The Returns of Investing in a Diversity Strategy

It's evident that diversity and inclusion efforts benefit the experiences of employees and team members who are part of marginalized groups. However, some people operate on the false belief that by supporting the rights of people in minority groups, they are "taking away" their own rights. They argue that women reporting sexual harassment could lead to extensive persecution for men, or that trying to hire a more diverse workforce will lead to more qualified white candidates being passed over. In truth, when diversity and inclusion strategies are actually implemented, people who are part of the majority demographic rarely suffer as much as they may have been led to believe through phobias or prejudices. In fact, the vast majority of people actually benefit from a more diverse group.

Diverse groups are often more efficient and effective than groups that are composed of only a single perspective. Companies can achieve greater success simply by working with more information. Having a diverse pool of employees to poll on various issues versus making decisions based on just one point of view is similar to the difference between learning a new topic by consuming various books, lectures, and videos, and watching only a single video on a topic before declaring yourself an expert. The fact of the matter is that you alone cannot know everything. You need to rely on others for help, and inviting diverse perspectives is the best way to do so. There is already a diversity of jobs in the workplace, with different responsibilities delegated to managers, HR staff, workers, accountants, and the CEO, each according to what they most excel at. Why not have this same level of diversity in the people filling these positions?

Diversity is a net gain for everyone involved, even though some may not believe this at first. Let's return to one of the previous two examples of resistance to greater diversity and see where the inaccuracies in these assumptions lie. First, consider the often-cited idea that better policies against sexual harassment could lead to discrimination for men. What are the implications of this statement? It seems to suggest one of two things: either there are men in the company who are constantly harassing women and these men's actions would be brought to light, or that women will go "mad with power" and start throwing around false accusations for innocent behaviors. If there are people committing sexual harassment in the company, it benefits everyone to remove them. This creates an unsafe work environment. The belief that women will take sexual harassment policies "too far" and use them as a punishment for men is demonstrably false. According to the U.S. National Sexual Violence Resource Center, "the prevalence of false reporting is between two percent and 10 percent" for claims of assault, which is far outweighed by "the majority of sexual assaults, an estimated 63 percent," which are "never reported to the police" (2012, p. 1-3). While exact statistics for workplace sexual harassment are harder to identify, as the definition of harassment can vary, along with the regularity at which it is reported, these numbers suggest that there are far more instances that go unreported or that are reported with no action taken than there are false reports. Since fears of false reports are largely exaggerated, more robust sexual harassment policies carry little harm for any group, and make the office a safer place as a whole.

Also, note that both of these assumptions are based on the idea that women are the harassed and men are the harassers. This is of course untrue, as women are just as capable of committing sexual harassment in the workplace as men. Better sexual harassment policies work to protect everyone, and they may even embolden men to speak up about harassment if they might have been too embarrassed to bring it up otherwise since these issues become destigmatized. Everyone benefits from a workplace free of harassment.

Inclusion and diversity policies have a significant positive impact, and they can improve the experiences of many people without leaving others at a disadvantage. Focusing on the great positive returns of investing in inclusion can help ease resistance and encourage everyone to work together to make the organization a more diversity-friendly space.

When looking into implementing diversity policies and getting your team excited about them, it helps to point out all the benefits they can provide. When everyone knows how policies will affect them and the health of the company, it's easier to bring everyone on board, since you can point to tangible and well-researched positive results.

Faster and More Effective Problem-Solving

You've probably had plenty of experiences where you've missed an obvious solution to a problem just because you weren't thinking about it the right way. If you're used to following a certain procedure for problem-solving, you can easily get stuck in your ways, disregarding possibly better alternatives in favor of sticking with what you've always done. While consistency can be useful in some situations, it's less helpful when compared with enhanced problem-solving methods you might enjoy if you improved the diversity of your team of problem-solvers.

A more diverse team can come up with solutions you never would have considered on your own. They might have a better idea of how to market to different demographics, have suggestions for streamlining processes you never considered, or provide feedback on your leadership style that can help you improve group morale and correct issues before they become bigger problems.

The Canadian Centre for Diversity and Inclusion published a series of case studies featuring businesses that have incorporated diversity and inclusion policies in their organizations. The Business Development Bank of Canada (BDC) was featured to highlight its program Entrepreneurship Connections to help newcomers to Canada start their own business and gain Canadian work experience. The program set a goal to help newcomers bring their skills and talent to the Canadian market. Throughout the course of the program, it became evident that,

> In developing the new program, BDC had been noticing that a growing number of people who were new to Canada were self-employed and that immigrants often were highly educated and came with a valuable understanding of global markets. BDC also saw that many were able to communicate in more than two languages and already had some social networks in place in Canada (van Ginkel 2016, p. 3).

They can even provide insights on further diversity measures, steering you away from more performative gestures that run the risk of alienating people and toward policies and decisions that will make a big difference for everyone at the office.

Greater diversity brings more ideas to the conversation, and inclusion allows the best ideas to rise to the top rather than getting buried under the same old problem-solving methods you've been using for years. Your organization can become faster and more efficient at every task, letting you accomplish more and reducing interpersonal conflicts that may otherwise occur along the way.

More Creativity and Innovation

Two people with different backgrounds and life experiences might look at the same situation and come away with very different interpretations. You can think of this like the Rorschach test, where people are presented with ink blots and asked to say what they see in them. Since there's no one correct answer, everyone could decide the same ink blot looks like something totally different. This is similar to what can happen within an organization when people with diverse perspectives tackle a project. With so many ideas and perspectives, there's more space for creative solutions and unique ways to tackle a project.

This increase in creativity can result in a lot of innovation for your company, and it may even help you get ahead of some of your competitors, offering products and services that others didn't even consider. Josh Bersin, a global research analyst for HR leadership issues, found that inclusive companies are "1.7 times more likely to be innovation leaders in their market," as well as significantly better at adapting to changes that impact workflow (2019, para. 15). Innovation is more common because there are more ideas to pull from. You can really stand out in your industry, all because you chose to listen to more voices.

Improved Engagement

Engagement is one of the most significant problems for any organization. How do you keep employees motivated so they can present their best work rather than phoning it in? How do you keep them around after the training period so you're not wasting time constantly training replacements? If you're holding meetings or running a charitable organization, how do you get people to keep coming back if there's no monetary gain for them? Engagement can be an especially big problem if you're just starting to recruit with diversity in mind, as people may find the culture hasn't yet adapted to having inclusive policies and may decide their time would be better spent elsewhere. This can be a serious problem, as your organization can become a "rotating door" where people seem to leave as quickly as they join the team. Diversity without inclusion breeds high turnover rates. The best way to prevent this is to prioritize inclusion efforts.

After taking part in a diversity and inclusion program at Blakes, Cassels & Graydon, a Canadian business law firm that has sought to have more diversity and inclusion within the legal community, a pre-law student had the following experience:

41

Amal said that before she was at the law firm, her expectation had been that women like her, identifying as a Muslim woman wearing a hijab, didn't pursue successful careers in law outside of their community. But a meeting with one of the lawyers at the firm who was a Muslim woman and a partner changed how she looked at a career in law and potential for a career at a large firm like Blakes unfolded for her (van Ginkel, 2017, p. 2).

Inclusive and diverse workforces have better employee retention because people enjoy their jobs. Discrimination is a big deciding factor in whether someone will keep a new job after the training period. If they feel like their coworkers and the higher-ups are treating them with prejudice, they're likely to walk right back out the door and find a job where they can feel respected. This means everyone's time has been wasted, including yours, the employees', the new hires' training team, and the people in charge of screening and interviewing in the hiring process. This also undermines confidence in your business if you're always looking for new employees. After a while, people are going to start wondering what kind of workplace conditions result in routine vacancies, and you may have a harder time finding qualified candidates. With inclusive policies, people feel valued and respected, so they're more likely to settle into the job, sticking around for years rather than mere weeks. This saves everyone time and money.

Additionally, the people who remain in the organization are likely to feel more engaged and motivated to work when they know their time isn't being wasted and they're not being disrespected. When everyone feels included, they're more engaged and willing to spend more time and effort on their projects. This is a huge benefit for everyone, as it cuts down on wasted time and a lack of productivity. Fellow team members feel like everyone is pulling their weight, meaning no one is taking on more than their fair share of work to make up for others, and managers see a marked increase in working speed and the quality of everyone's output. It's a win-win scenario, all thanks to diversity and inclusion efforts.

Increased Profits

With increases in productivity and output come increases in a company's profits. More diverse workplaces have generally seen higher profits, in part due to higher employee morale alongside other factors like innovation, a more complete understanding of diverse markets, reduced resources spent thanks to lower rates of employee turnover, and greater appeal to potential customers thanks to their inclusion efforts. Research conducted across diverse and non-diverse companies in Canada found that "companies with the most ethnically/culturally diverse boards worldwide are 43% more likely to experience higher profits" (Canadian Construction Association, 2019, p. 8). Similar studies in the U.S.

have reported similar, if not higher, likelihoods of improving profits. Even non-profits and more casual groups like clubs and sports teams can improve their effectiveness by introducing diversity, whether they're better able to fundraise across different demographics, increase awareness and incite more significant change for a charitable or social cause, or simply improve their performance. Diversity is a smart move for raising your bottom line, and it can help you pull ahead in your market no matter what the goals of your group are.

In a company, profit increases typically benefit the people at the top of the ladder most, so they're the most likely to approve of the new diversity measures. As the leader of your organization, you stand to gain the most from a more productive company, as do any investors who make a portion of your profits. Many company higher-ups enjoy performance-based bonuses, so these profit increases will be favorable to them as well. Of course, you can spread these profit increases out so regular employees benefit from them too. You might offer company-wide bonuses or raises when the company is especially successful, which motivates everyone to work together and get more high-quality work done as a result. You can also show your appreciation to your employees through company parties and similar recognition events. This way, everyone gets to benefit from increased profits, therefore workers at all levels see how diversity and inclusion policies can directly benefit them.

Improved Company Reputation

Your organization's reputation can have a significant impact on your success. If potential customers boycott your products and services or you can't get the word out about new development or have issues because people don't trust your brand, you stand to lose a lot in terms of profits and the effectiveness of your efforts. A smaller reach is bad for any organization, and it could eventually lead to the closure of your group or company if you can no longer generate support. The good news is that great diversity and inclusion policies can really improve your company's image, with some powerful results.

It is very difficult to build brand loyalty when there are notable inequalities lurking beneath the surface of a company's operations, especially in younger demographics. Brand loyalty is a persistent commitment to your products and services, often to the extent that people would choose to pay more for them simply because they like your brand. Consider the case of products that use fair trade-sourced labor and goods rather than relying on underpaid work or child labor. These products typically cost more to buy at the store, yet many companies like Ben & Jerry's or Green Mountain coffee remain successful because their policies have cultivated brand loyalty in their consumers. On the other hand, companies that make no move to diversify and continue to support labor exploitation may soon find themselves losing their footholds in the market. Thanks to the growing public consciousness over issues of class and race in production and company management, "More than ever consumers are cognizant of firms endorsing child labor in foreign countries, of preserving homogenous board rooms, or of blatantly violating human and social rights. Brand loyalty is the direct result of favorable psychological and emotional impressions that the corporate image evokes" (Phillipe, 2011, para. 8). If this corporate image is steeped in human rights violations and discriminatory policies, people may avoid using your services. If your brand comes across as a leader in inclusive efforts, you're more likely to draw in more customers, which leads to more sales and helps attract great job candidates.

Overall, the returns of diversity and inclusion policies are widespread, and in many cases they're returns you don't want to risk missing out on. They can be a huge benefit to your organization in more ways than one. If you're looking to improve morale, support productivity, increase creativity and innovation, and build a supportive base of customers or listeners, inclusivity should be one of your greatest priorities.

Chapter 5: Challenges of Inclusive Leadership

A diverse workplace comes with many unique challenges. Cultural and procedural differences run the risk of interfering with the collaborative process, which can in turn slow workflow. Conflicts may arise at points of difference, and if they're not managed in a way that shows respect to everyone involved, they could lead to significant divisions within your team. Adopting inclusive leadership strategies also means being willing to navigate the complex challenges that a diverse, inclusive group poses. You'll need to put your conflict resolution skills to the test from time to time, but if you handle these challenges well, you'll be rewarded with an exceptional team of diverse minds all working together to achieve a common goal. This is an invaluable tool, so it's well worth managing these occasional bumps in the road.

The challenges of inclusive leadership can come in a variety of different forms. Diverse perspectives can lead to differences in opinion on how to tackle an issue. For example, some may take a more traditional approach while others want to innovate. Each person may be used to doing things a different way according to their culture and background, and it can be hard to devise a solution that doesn't alienate one person or the other. There's also the difficulty of making sure everyone feels included. If you put up decorations for the winter holidays, you may only think to decorate according to the holidays celebrated by your religion, while unthinkingly neglecting others. Many businesses put out Christmas decorations but don't allow employees to display Chanukah decorations, seeing them as more religiously affiliated just because Christmas is more prevalent in North American culture. Eid, Diwali or Kwanzaa-inclusive decorations are even more rarely seen. Other inclusivity issues can be as subtle as throwing a work party but having only alcoholic drinks available, so those who choose not to drink don't have anything available. These issues may not be directly related to the work performed by your organization, but they can affect peoples' morale and leave them feeling less valued than some of their coworkers.

To be a truly inclusive leader, it's important to account for these potential challenges and do your best to address them. In this chapter, we'll look at some of the most common difficulties that can arise when trying to create a diverse and inclusive workforce. These include a reliance on stereotypes when trying to account for different groups, a tendency to look for commonalities with team members that can lead to exclusion, the prevalence of ethnocentrism, and the tendency for some to perceive diversity as a threat. While these are a good place to start, it's possible you may encounter other conflicts that don't fit neatly into any of these categories. In these situations, it's best to practice mindful listening as a conflict resolution skill. Be open about asking team members to come to you when they have a disagreement with someone else or a concern about how the group is run, and try to see their perspective of the issue. This will put you in the best possible position to address it effectively and support your team.

Reliance on Stereotypes

Even when you are doing your best to be inclusive, there may be times when you accidentally find yourself buying into rhetoric that characterizes people from different groups as all acting a certain way. For example, some people believe that women are naturally better at dealing with emotional issues, or that they're more maternal and therefore they should spend more time at home with their kids and less time at the office. Of course, this kind of thinking doesn't account for the thousands of women who aren't interested in having kids, or who have worked hard to balance their home life and their careers. It is simply a stereotype, and putting too much faith in it can make it harder to help women feel fully integrated into the group.

It's important to note that there is no such thing as a beneficial stereotype. Some stereotypes suggest that a certain group is superior in some way or another; as an example, many people believe that Asian people are more skilled in math or smarter overall. While this is considered a positive stereotype, it is positive in name alone, and can actually still cause just as much harm as a negative stereotype. If you constantly insist that an Asian employee should deal with the company's finances, even if this wasn't the job they were hired to perform, you unfairly burden them with an expectation you likely wouldn't give to anyone else. They feel more pressure to perform well in a role they may or may not be good at, and in a sense, their status as an individual is replaced with a broad-strokes caricature of their identity. Another supposedly-positive racial stereotype, that of the "strong black woman," is even clearer in its potential to cause harm. Believing that black women can and should tolerate greater injustice and harsher conditions than their white, male peers means you may take their concerns less seriously and leave them to perform more difficult work, which isn't fair or equitable. At the end of the day, any generalization applied to an entire group is bound to be incorrect about many of its members, and all of these generalizations have the potential to do harm.

Rejecting Stereotypes by Viewing the Individual

How do you combat the tendency to rely heavily on stereotypes? The best way is to accept that every person is an individual with their own thoughts and feelings, and acknowledge that their membership in a racial, cultural, ethnic, or religious group is just one part of them, not their defining characteristic. There is no demographic where all people included in the demographic act the same. While many people of color hold liberal values, plenty are more conservative. While many men are into sports and cars, others have no interest in these topics and prefer hobbies like baking and painting. While many Christians consider their religious values to be a significant part of who they are, others may only occasionally attend Sunday mass and have values that deviate from typically Christian ones, while still considering themselves part of the faith. Engage people on an individual, personal level. Don't boil them down to their demographics.

The easiest method for seeing people of different backgrounds as real people and not just stand-ins for their culture is to spend time with them, getting to know who they are and what they enjoy. Collaborate directly with them on projects. Invite everyone to spend time together with team building exercises and fun non-work events. The more opportunities you and other members of the team have to get to know each other as people, the less you'll find yourself relying on stereotypes to fill in the gaps.

The Like-Me Bias

A few years ago, the company Airbnb, which is based around connecting people looking to rent out their houses and spare rooms with people looking to find accommodations, had an issue with their hiring process. There was very little diversity in who they hired, and it was starting to become a very apparent problem. At that time, hiring managers were instructed to find commonalities with the candidates they were interviewing. They would review a resume, looking at the listed skills and hobbies, and open their interviews by speaking about an interest they had in common. Ideally, this was meant to create a more welcoming, relaxed atmosphere and present Airbnb as a friendly place to work. In practice, it had the exact opposite effect, and actually led to a decrease in diverse employees.

How did this happen? The answer lies in the phenomena known as the "like-me bias" or "similar-to-me bias," which suggests that people tend to prefer interacting with those they see as similar to themselves. When considered under the lens of hiring employees, it's clear to see how so many companies end up with non-diverse workforces if there is no specific push to increase diversity. The like-me bias can apply to race, religion, sexual orientation, gender, class, and yes, even to hobbies. What Airbnb found with their old policy was that "If you're only connecting with people who share your background and experiences, you'll end up hiring people exactly like you. And what happens to the candidates you have nothing in common with? That person who's the polar opposite of you might be fantastic in the role, but subconsciously you're already writing them off as a bad fit" (McLaren, 2017, para. 24). This stands in direct opposition to the foundational tenets of most diversity strategies, which are all about actively seeking out different opinions and lifestyles. When you only look for people who are like you, you run the risk of excluding anyone who isn't similar enough, which can muddy the waters of inclusivity efforts.

Embracing Differences and Standardizing Hiring Criteria

To counteract the harmful effects of the like-me bias, it's useful to adopt hiring strategies that support and praise differences. If you're making an active effort to invite more diverse people to your team, you're already starting to shift your mind toward seeing dissimilarities as advantages, but don't stop there. Instead of trying to connect with people based on similarities, you might pivot and show interest in hobbies and skills that are unique. Ask questions about how someone's experiences and their point of view have taught them important lessons, and even what they would change about the company they're applying for if they could. This has the added benefit of being a great way to get feedback from someone outside the company that reflects public perception of the way your business operates, which can also assist in your efforts to target diversity. Working to recognize and unlearn your unconscious biases is another key step in reworking your hiring process. Unconscious biases will be covered in more detail in Chapter 7.

A great way to avoid the like-me bias in hiring is to have a standard set of criteria when evaluating potential candidates. This is exactly the solution

Airbnb chose when they realized their old policy was disproportionately working to homogenize the company. Standardized criteria should include categories for assessment that are neutral and emphasize someone's suitability for the job rather than focusing on less important things like hobbies and home lives. For example, if you're looking to hire a new accountant, you might ask your interviewer to evaluate candidates' education, their responses to "what would you do"-style questions depicting different scenarios at work, and what they believe each candidate could bring to the table that isn't already present at the company. These kinds of criteria work to normalize differences as well, holding up the belief that diversity is what makes the company really stand out, not widespread similarities.

Ethnocentric Thinking

Ethnocentrism refers to the tendency to view others' behaviors and practices through your own cultural lens. You understand your own values best, which can sometimes make it difficult to accept people who have different values than you. Oftentimes, ethnocentrism can lead to you seeing your own culture as the "correct" one and the cultures of others as "foreign" and "strange." In some cases, you may be tempted to see others' ways of life and choices as "backwards" compared to your own. While you may not intend to view other people through this lens, it's frequently a bad habit that's hard to break, as these observations can sometimes happen without you noticing you're making them.

Ethnocentric thinking can be harmful because it causes you to think of the practices of others as unusual, painting them in a negative light. Rather than accepting that people from different backgrounds have their own ways of life that may differ from yours, you may attempt to correct these differences, imposing your values on others. This can quickly turn into judgments based on prejudice.

Overcoming Ethnocentrism

To a certain extent, you are always going to be somewhat influenced by the culture you grew up in. You may find that you don't fully understand the behaviors of people from other ethnic groups largely because you lack the cultural context that turns much of what you might see as odd into a commonplace occurrence. Therefore, overcoming ethnocentrism typically starts with learning more about other cultures. The better you understand how people live in different countries or even among different racial, ethnic, or cultural groups, the easier it becomes to see the people in these groups as fellow humans whose practices deserve as much dignity and respect as your own. If you have a gut negative reaction to seeing a behavior you're not familiar with, consider why you might feel this way. Is there anything actually wrong or harmful about the behavior, or does your confusion stem from ethnocentric perceptions of how people "should" act? Performing these little mental corrections routinely can help you reframe these interactions and catch yourself before you make an unfair assumption about someone else's culture.

Confusing Diversity with Replacement or Erasure

One of the biggest barriers to creating a diverse and inclusive workforce is the prevalence of the "fear of replacement" that can often pervade the majority demographic. When people are used to being in charge and having more privilege than others, they may see people in minority groups being granted these same privileges as a threat to their own. Consider how many people view gay marriage as an attack on heterosexual couples' marriages, when in actually there is little to no impact on straight peoples' ability to marry. There is no risk of the erasure of marriage between a man and a woman, nor is there a way for the acceptance of gay marriage to "ruin the sanctity of marriage," and yet this type of thinking is one of the most commonly-cited anti-gay marriage arguments.

The fear of replacement can be especially pervasive in the workplace because there are only a certain number of jobs that need to be filled at any given company. If more jobs go to people in minority groups, then it follows that fewer positions might be filled by people who are straight, white, male, or able-bodied. Some may fear that they could lose their job simply for not being diverse enough. Of course, in practice most diversity policies focus on hiring more diverse people, not firing people, yet this fear still persists in many workplaces. If left to linger, it can lead to resentment toward minority employees that culminates in harassment and exclusion. It is especially important to address these issues as soon as you think they are occurring to prevent them from boiling over into serious tensions in the group.

Eliminating the "Us Versus Them" Mentality

What you may have noticed about this particular form of prejudice is that it is based on the idea that there is a clear differentiation between an in-group and an out-group. The underlying statement here can be summed up by the phrase "they will not replace us," which is also a phrase used by many white nationalist groups. This is no coincidence. At the core of this statement is the belief that there is an "us" and a "them," and that the two cannot coexist. In other words, the fear of replacement is based on an inherently divisive view of the world that suggests that people from different demographic groups cannot have positive interactions with each other. Therefore, the key to abolishing this line of thinking in the workplace is to eliminate these categories of "us" and "them" and instead help employees see everyone in the group as part of a whole team.

If you notice people are resistant to the idea of diversity, start off by listening to their concerns. Try to figure out what exactly they're afraid of, and explain that the company becoming more diverse will not lead to losing their job or devaluing them as employees. Make it clear that you're trying to help everyone with these measures. You can even use the diversity benefits discussed in Chapter 4 to explain why a more inclusive workplace is actually beneficial to the whole team.

It's also good practice to include a few people who may initially resist diversity in some aspects of your diversity initiative. Too often people can be made to feel like they're being tossed aside as your focus pivots to minority employees. They may also be unclear about what exactly your diversity strategy entails, and they may fill in their knowledge gaps with assumptions that you're giving others preferential treatment. By including them in the process, you can show them exactly what steps you're taking to make the workplace more diverse, dispelling any preconceived notions. You also continue to include them in your new program, which demonstrates how these programs are about inclusion for everyone, not just people who are part of minority groups. Additionally, you avoid the problem of expecting people in minority groups to do all the work to correct bias and inclusivity issues while still allowing them to have their voices heard. By getting dissenters to work together on a team with people who are genuinely excited for the group's new diversity initiative, you break down some of the barriers dividing these groups and encourage cooperation.

Using this method comes with the caveat that these teams should be supervised and ideally led by someone with experience in working within a diverse team. Diversity efforts backfire if they become an excuse to pair people of color with someone who may not show them respect, expecting them to take on the burden of eliminating prejudices. If people in the group feel uncomfortable or unsafe, you may need to intervene directly or, in some cases, consider letting an employee go if they cannot act respectfully. It's never ideal to lose a team member for these reasons, but your workplace cannot be inclusive if there are people actively working to undermine that inclusivity and perpetuate toxic behaviors. Everyone must feel safe in order for diversity and inclusion protocols to be considered successful. For a leader, the safety of your team members should always be your top priority.

Chapter 6: Diversity and Inclusion as a Core Leadership Competency

Despite the recent push for many businesses and organizations to adopt more robust diversity policies, these skills haven't typically been highly valued as leadership skills in the past. Think about what a typical course selection might look like for a business major in college who someday wants to lead their own company. What sort of classes would you expect to find? You might see courses like marketing, finance, negotiation, and entrepreneurship, which are all considered to be core competencies for leaders. They may have classes teaching them how to be a more effective leader that focus on the internal structure of a company, finding a mentor, or improving their communication skills. However, chances are fairly slim that you'll see any courses about how to deal with diversity in the office outside of a few select universities. While many of the previously mentioned skills are important for leaders, diversity is consistently undervalued in comparison, to the extent that it is rarely even taught to aspiring CEOs.

If you consider typical leadership advice, this trend holds true. Values like charisma, the ability to command respect, and effective motivation techniques are frequently mentioned, but many pass over the equally beneficial advice of improving one's knowledge of diversity and inclusion-related concerns. Why is it that diversity so often gets passed over in favor of other leadership competencies? One potential reason is that many believe diversity isn't integral to a company's success. As you have seen in previous chapters, diversity can have very significant benefits for your company, so this isn't quite true, even if some people in the industry are slow to recognize this.

Another reason is that some leaders may not recognize the need to be intentional about diversity and inclusion efforts. Since diversity trends upward over time, diversity within companies generally increases as well, even in lieu of targeted diversity movements. However, this isn't the same as adopting real inclusive policies. Company diversity may increase, but on the whole employees from minority groups hold fewer administrative and management positions, and even an increase in diversity doesn't guarantee the company will be any more inclusive of their differences.

Additionally, some people just don't see a problem in need of correcting. Many people have never had to face discrimination in their lives, so they don't recognize the ways it can influence and harm people who have to fight to be included. These leaders may also shrug off disputes or reports of inappropriate behavior as employee bickering rather than taking the matter seriously, and in doing so, fail to recognize how many of these conflicts are only able to slow work speed down because they stem from biases prevalent throughout the company hierarchy.

Even though diversity and inclusion training so rarely get the respect it deserves, leaders need to learn and practice these skills to be truly effective. Without them, organizations suffer from a lack of significant diversity, fewer advantages in problem-solving and innovation, and more frequent conflicts from mismanaged and nonexistent inclusivity policies. At the end of the day, diversity and inclusion skills are just another part of managing your team, and they're critical for success.

To better understand how these initiatives fit into the more commonly recognized core leadership competencies, we'll first take a look at those competencies as they're currently defined. Then we'll consider how integration initiatives can be included alongside them.

Understanding Leadership Competencies

A leadership competency is a skill or style of management that improves the volume and quality of your team's work output. These kinds of skills are valuable for every single leader to know, since they benefit everyone involved.

Given this definition, it's not hard to see how diversity and inclusion fit into this mold. As we've already discussed, leaders who are well-versed in these two skills are excellent at getting the best from their teams because biases and prejudices don't hold the team back. There are fewer conflicts, teams have improved problem-solving skills thanks to so many people with diverse perspectives offering their advice, and the team is highly motivated. It is becoming undeniable that diversity and inclusion should now be considered just as important as the more commonly agreed-upon leadership competencies. Even though they are relatively new concerns for most employers and organization leaders, they have more than proven their worthiness of being recognized as basic competencies that are widely taught to new and upcoming leaders.

Treating Diversity and Inclusion as Core Competencies

Diversity and inclusion efforts do a great deal to improve communication and quality of life for team members. Therefore, they should be of paramount importance to any leader. It is as important to invest in these efforts as it is to learn proper budgeting, organizational management, and conflict management skills. However, since these skills aren't often given the respect they deserve as core competencies, you may need to take the time to educate yourself rather than relying on already existing programs. Whether you graduated with honors from a business school or you began your organization as a small friend group with no prior experience, you'll need to take a few extra steps to ensure diversity and inclusion is a core part of your leadership strategy. Some good starting points are furthering your education, putting yourself at the forefront of all diversity and inclusion efforts, and taking responsibility for any issues that may arise while working to correct them.

Pursue Your Own Education

Since diversity and inclusion is often left out of the conversation of core leadership competencies, you may need to educate yourself outside of a classroom, mentorship program, or leadership training course. The more you learn about not just inclusivity initiatives but also about the cultures and lifestyles of people different from you, the better off you will be as an inclusive leader.

Of course, you've already taken the first steps in educating yourself by picking up this book, which is a great start. As you continue to read, consider how each tip and idea within this book applies to your current leadership style and your organization. Ask yourself frequently how you would go about implementing real change within your group, carrying out the strategies presented here.

Even once you've finished this book, there's still plenty to learn. While we cover the process and important values involved in leading with inclusivity in mind, you may feel the need to do additional research to reinforce what you've read and expand upon some subjects. It's also a good idea to learn about the unique social and cultural differences different demographics face so you can be better prepared to implement policies that account for these differences. For example, it's great to expand religious inclusion efforts to give Jewish employees the holidays off, but you'll find it very hard to do so without learning about these holidays and what significance each of them holds. Spend some time learning more about people who lead very different lives from your own. In addition to improving your leadership skills, you'll also be more knowledgeable about your team members and better able to empathize with the different perspectives of everyone who works for you.

Don't Delegate Excessively

It can be very tempting to set up a taskforce for dealing with diversity and inclusion matters and then sit back and let them work. Delegation can be helpful in some regards, but it shouldn't be the extent of the work you put into remedying inclusivity issues. When you do this, you put the burden of fixing problems on the people who experience the negative effects of the problems the most keenly. Not only is this unfair, it also showcases a lack of leadership, as you aren't willing to pave the way to a better company culture yourself.

It's not a bad idea to create a specific task force for ensuring everyone feels included and coming up with policies to deal with any problems team members are experiencing, but if you do, make sure to remain a key player in the task force. Don't sit back and let other people take the reins. Get directly involved, whether through asking for feedback about the current inclusivity policies, actively encouraging conversations about discrimination, or coming up with new measures that could benefit the company. Your team shouldn't feel like they've been left to deal with these issues alone. In addition to showing support and leading the charge for inclusivity, you'll learn much more about the specific problems people in your organization are facing if you take the time to personally speak with them.

Take Responsibility for Inclusion Issues

If someone on your team reports an instance of discrimination, it can sometimes be tempting to find fault in everyone except yourself. After all, you're actively trying to fix these issues, and if you're not the one who said or did something motivated by prejudice then it couldn't possibly be your fault, right? Unfortunately, as well-intentioned as you might be, you are the leader of your organization, which means you are ultimately responsible for the behaviors you permit everyone to engage in. These actions happen under your watch, whether you yourself committed them or not. Therefore, take a proactive role in examining what shortcomings led to this discrimination event occurring and what you can do to prevent it from happening again in the future. The worst thing you can do in this situation is expect the person reporting the incident to fix it themselves by changing their behavior or attitude, as this communicates that you're not taking their concerns seriously and you're unwilling to stand by their side. When prejudice takes root in your company, recognize your role in allowing it to continue, and correct the issue as soon as possible.

Chapter 7: What Is Unconscious Bias?

We've mentioned unconscious bias a few times in the book so far, but what exactly is it? As you likely already know, bias is a predisposition that causes you to react positively or negatively to something, regardless of the actual interaction you have. When discussing issues of diversity, bias is typically negative, reflective prejudices against certain racial or ethnic groups. However, it can sometimes be positive, making you more likely to side with certain members of the company in disputes or more likely to offer them raises because of your bias toward people in your own racial group. In some cases, it is easy to recognize when bias clouds your judgment. Conscious bias is intentional. When you engage in it, you may be thinking something along the lines of, "this person isn't like me," therefore justifying your negative perception of them to yourself. Conscious bias can be harmful, of course, but since you can easily recognize when it occurs, it's easier to correct than your unconscious biases.

Unconscious bias is, as the name suggests, not as immediately recognizable. You don't always notice you're engaging in it, nor do you realize how it affects your actions unless you're frequently practicing self-reflection. Unconscious biases result in people who don't consider themselves to be racist, and who may even try to be actively anti-racist, continuing to perpetuate stereotypes with carelessly discriminatory words and actions without recognizing the harm they're causing. This can make it especially difficult to correct because if you are called out on a bias you didn't know you were acting on, your first thought might be to get defensive rather than to listen to the criticism.

Unconscious biases can be hard to fix, but it's far from impossible. The greatest tool in your arsenal here is knowledge. The more you know about biases and where they're most likely to occur, the better you'll be at identifying when they're clouding your judgment. In this chapter, we'll start off by looking at a few common types of unconscious biases. Then we'll discuss methods for correcting them.

Examples of Unconscious Biases

In Chapter 5, we took a look at the dangers of the like-me bias and the difficulties it can pose for your organization. The like-me bias is just one example of an unconscious bias, and it's far from the only one. Biases can crop up in unexpected places and seriously harm the integrity of the group if they're left unchecked. Identifying them and learning when to call them out, whether they're your own biases or the biases of your team members, can help immensely in eliminating prejudice within the group or workplace.

To be effective at recognizing bias, you'll need to know exactly what you're looking for. Bias can occur in many different situations, and some are especially common within workforces. Three notable unconscious biases that can negatively affect the company are rigid ideas about gender roles, the horn and halo effect, and confirmation bias.

Gender Roles

Gender roles are social and cultural ideas about the supposedly-naturally occurring strengths and weaknesses of each gender. Throughout North America, gender roles are fairly pervasive, as most people are taught to believe in them from a very young age. Little girls get princess costumes and baby dolls as toys, while boys get race cars and dinosaurs. Of course, given the opportunity to choose their own toys, some girls would probably be happier to stage a fight with dinosaur toys, and some boys would enjoy throwing a tea party just as much as girls. However, rigid concepts of what gender is and how people of different genders should act can pigeonhole children into sticking to stereotypically masculine and feminine activities, and these ideas about gender become harder to break as kids grow older and are taught not to question them.

In Western society, especially strict ideas about gender roles are common. The West tends to expect women to put their home lives over their careers and personal goals. Women are expected to stay home with kids and prioritize getting married, while most people wouldn't bat an eye at an unmarried man in his 40s or a father who spends more time at work than he does at home. It's also common for assertive behaviors to be labeled as "bossy" in women while being desirable traits for male leaders. Gender roles also come with the complication of failing to account for people outside of the gender binary or trans individuals, who don't fit neatly into the boxes society has created for men and women. Nonbinary team members may struggle to find a place they fit in if their workplace or organization is heavily entrenched in gender roles, and trans men and women may face greater discrimination for not "fitting into" their assigned roles.

Gender roles can have a direct impact on how you react to the same task performed by different genders. You might evaluate women and men differently for an upper management position because you've been conditioned to see men as more dominant and professionally successful, and therefore more likely to hold positions of power. You may look more critically at women who are driven and focused on their careers with no desire to raise a family anytime soon than you would for men prioritizing their jobs over their personal relationships. Additionally, many of the traits commonly associated with leaders and administrators, like confidence and assertiveness, don't mesh well with the gender roles women are expected to perform in society. This can have significant consequences for their upward mobility within an organization. One study found that in team evaluations, the phrases "abrasive" and "too aggressive" appeared almost exclusively in women's evaluations, and "87.9 percent of women received critical feedback compared to 58.9 percent of men." On top of this, critiques for men were "heavily geared towards suggestions for additional skills to develop," while women were told to "quiet down and step back" (Ellevate Network, 2015, para. 5-6). These kinds of suggestions can interfere with women's ability to succeed, even when they're performing similarly to their male peers.

The Horn and Halo Effect

The horn and halo effect is a type of unconscious bias where a single trait colors your perception of a person or situation. In the horn effect, the trait is negative, and your mind casts a negative light on everything else someone does. For example, if you find someone to be rude, you might perceive insult from all future interactions with them and quietly root against them in your mind. You may find that small things like whistling or tapping a pencil against the desk bother you, even when you could easily brush these minor annoyances off if they were committed by anyone else. On the other hand, the halo effect is the exact opposite. A single positive trait comes to define someone, and you overlook all the bad things they do in favor of their best aspects. For example, if someone helps you out with a project or they share one of your hobbies, you might overlook future poor job performance and other issues. The horn and halo effect boils our perceptions of people down into just one interaction or characteristic, which prevents us from seeing them as real people, with both good and bad traits.

Allowing the horn and halo effect to persist can have negative consequences for your organization. You may be slower to address issues within the workplace if you feel like you have to discipline someone you like. You may be more likely to recognize one person's work on a project over the contributions of everyone else, and you may end up giving someone a promotion who might not deserve it compared to the amount of work other team members have done. The horn effect can lead you to be unfairly critical of a single person, to the point that they may consider quitting just to avoid feeling persecuted in the workplace. When combined with issues of racial prejudice and discrimination, the horn and halo effect can perpetuate these negative systems. You may find yourself acting more favorably toward someone from your own race, excusing their faults and more readily praising them, and being overly harsh on someone you don't have the same connection with. When trying to eliminate the horn and halo effect, it's critical to remember that people are complex and have many strengths and weaknesses. It does you no good to overlook someone's weaknesses in favor of a single strength, nor does it help you to overlook their strengths because of just one weakness. Recognize the whole person, not just one or two traits, so you can help everyone play to their strengths and ensure all team members are being treated equally.

Confirmation Bias

Confirmation bias is another way of saying that you believe what you want to be true. It's a tendency to jump to conclusions that support your initial assessment of a situation, either without knowing all the facts or by actively disregarding any evidence to the contrary. If you want something to be true, you're more likely to believe evidence in favor of it, and less likely to believe evidence that suggests it might not be true. Even if you try to be an objective observer, your tendency toward confirmation bias can lead you astray. Confirmation bias can happen on all sides of a given issue. For example, people who do not already value diversity may cite studies of workplace conflicts and use their fears of losing their jobs to disregard the overwhelming evidence that a more diverse workplace has net gains for everyone. On the other hand, people who believe very strongly in diversity may brush aside the actual conflicts that do occur in a more diverse workplace, unknowingly making these conflicts worse by refusing to admit they exist at all. This type of unconscious bias is dangerous because it blinds you to the truth of the situation, good or bad, and interferes with your ability to recognize and accept viewpoints different from your own.

Confirmation bias typically has the strongest negative effects in the hiring process. First impressions are very important to your overall perception of a candidate. A great first impression could blind you to other flaws that make a candidate a less-than-ideal fit for your company, and a bad first impression that has been tainted by bias can lead you to ignore a perfectly good candidate in favor of a less experienced one. If one candidate is more charismatic than the others, you might subconsciously decide they're the right fit for your company, even though they may lack some important qualifications. This can cause you to pass over people who might deserve the job more just because they didn't fit into your predetermined idea of how a model employee looks and acts. When combined with prejudices, this can result in less diversity in new employees as you no longer evaluate every candidate on an even playing field.

In addition to being a potential issue for hiring managers, confirmation bias can kick in any time the group is working collaboratively to solve a problem. Let's say you run a company that has been doing marketing the same way forever. You're hesitant to overhaul your marketing department because you don't want to go through all the extra effort if the results aren't significantly improved. Therefore, you might go into any trials of a new system with a negative bias, focusing on all the places the untested system still has kinks to iron out and ignoring the fact that it's a new system and it isn't going to be perfect on the first try. You're more likely to overlook the ways in which a new strategy benefits the company, instead focusing on the positives of the old strategy. In effect, you've decided the old way of doing something is better before you've given the new way a shot. This is part of the reason why a lot of companies are resistant to change, even if updating policies and strategies could save them a lot of time and money in the long run. Watch out for confirmation bias when you're trying to come up with new solutions to old problems, and give every idea a fair shot if it seems promising. You might be surprised how much better the results look if you let yourself look at them with an open mind.

How to Recognize and Eliminate Unconscious Biases

Recognition is the first and most important step in reducing the power of unconscious biases. Since these biases live in your subconscious and you may act on them almost out of instinct, they're hard to root out and easy to ignore or excuse. You now know some of the most common examples of unconscious bias, so you have a good idea of when you should start paying attention to your motivations and questioning whether they might be the result of unchecked biases. As you work to combat the role unconscious bias can have in your organization, focus on identifying the situations where these examples are most likely to occur. For example, pay special attention to your hiring managers and sit in on a few interviews. Look over employee evaluations and consider whether some evaluations sound notably harsher than others. When discussing possible changes to the way the organization operates, make sure the conversation steers clear of instances of confirmation bias. Then you can push back against your biases by working to recognize their harm and gently correcting yourself and your team members when bias arises.

Consider the harm done rather than the harm intended. When people are accused of acting with bias, they tend to get defensive about their actions. It's a natural response. After all, you might tell yourself you didn't mean to do anything wrong. You might have even been trying to be inclusive and you said or did the wrong thing. Maybe you don't understand why someone might be angry over a small mistake, or even something you don't see as harmful from your point of view. Whatever your internal rationalization, it's easy to become mad in this kind of situation. You default to frustration in part because you feel like you're being unfairly blamed for something you didn't intend to happen.

While that may be true, it's also true that intentions don't always matter as much as you might like. If you're carrying a glass of red wine and you trip and spill the wine all over someone's white dress, does it matter whether or not you intended to spill it? To some extent, the unfortunate recipient of the spill might be more willing to forgive you, but the wine-colored stain on their dress will remain whether or not it was really an accident. There are consequences for an act of carelessness, just as there are consequences for an act of maliciousness, and some of these consequences may overlap.

Careless acts of prejudice can have similar results, leaving a "stain" behind even if everyone involved is willing to forgive and forget for the most part. This stain can discolor future interactions, casting them in a more negative light. This is especially likely if you're not willing to accept the role you played or to take measures to correct your behavior, since nothing about your ability to recognize unconscious biases will change.

How can you avoid this tendency to get defensive and instead make real steps toward preventing the issue from happening again? First, remind yourself that not meaning to do something is not the same as not doing it. Even if you didn't mean to hurt someone, you might have done so anyway. Try to think of the situation from their perspective, and consider what you'd like to see happen if you were them. At the very least, you'd probably want a genuine apology, and for the person who unknowingly hurt you to take steps to prevent it from happening again. You'll have a tough time changing your behavior if you refuse to recognize it in the first place. Have conversations, ask what exactly you did that made others feel hurt, and remember this next time an unconscious bias rears its ugly head.

As you start to recognize harm done rather than harm intended, your immediate response to unconscious bias shifts from "I didn't mean to do that, so it's not my fault you got hurt" to "I didn't mean to do that, but I recognize it was harmful anyway and I'll avoid doing it again in the future." You're more likely to catch yourself before similar instances of unconscious bias interference can occur again because you know what kind of behaviors hurt others and you're treating them seriously.

Internalized Biases

Not all of your biases may be directed at other groups of people. You may hold some biases about people who share your race, ethnic group, gender, sexual orientation, disability, or religion. This is usually the result of hearing a stereotype repeatedly over the years and eventually coming to believe it about yourself or others like you. These are known as internalized biases, and they can have powerful negative effects on your thoughts and behaviors. In extreme cases, they can lead to self-hatred, stress, and mental health issues, as they undermine your self-confidence and leave you feeling lost about your own identity.

The more we are exposed to an idea, the more likely it is to take root in our minds. It goes from something unbelievable to something we're used to encountering, even if we're skeptical of it, until we may find ourselves starting to believe it. This is exactly how internalized biases work. Consider the example of the "sassy black woman" stereotype, which suggests that black women are on average louder, cruder, angrier, and often more malicious than white women or even black men. Of course, this is just a stereotype, but many black women have grown up exposed to this idea their whole lives, both in pop culture and in conversations in the real world. Eventually, they may start to put some stock in such a frequently recounted idea, and they may start changing their own behaviors so they can't be accused of fitting the stereotype. They may start speaking softer and less often, even though it means their perspective isn't adequately represented in discussions. They may soften their words and put up with more unfair treatment because they don't want to cause a problem. Then they can point at themselves and say, "See? I'm not like them. If other black women acted like I do, there wouldn't be a problem." This undermines the role bias and prejudice plays in creating these false perceptions of different groups, forces black women to take up less space in conversations in order to separate themselves from the "sassy" label, and cultivates resentment between black women.

As you practice the above methods for recognizing unconscious biases, pay attention to internalized biases too. Remember that you are an individual, and that stereotypes about any group you may belong to do not define who you are and how you are allowed to act. Give yourself permission to be your true, authentic self.

Chapter 8: What Are Microaggressions?

It is very easy to take a firm stance against obvious acts of racism. If someone uses inappropriate language like slurs, you can correct them, as this is inexcusable in any organization. If there is clear, unfair targeting of a specific employee because of their race, religion, ethnicity, sexual orientation, disability, class, or another aspect of their identity, it's readily apparent that there's a problem in need of fixing. If there is a pay gap between white male employees and employees who are female or people of color, you can see the disparity very clearly, which makes it easier to correct. Addressing diversity and inclusion is never a walk in the park, but it's easier to identify and put a stop to more obvious forms of racism, sexism, homophobia, ableism, and other types of prejudice. But what happens when prejudice flies under the radar thanks to obfuscating language or more minor but still harmful offenses? It can be much more difficult to get everyone to agree discrimination is even happening and that it should be taken seriously in these cases, let alone actually stopping it. This is the hidden danger of microaggressions.

According to the American Psychological Association, Columbia University psychology professor Derald Wing Sue, PhD, defines microaggressions as "everyday insults, indignities and demeaning messages sent to people of color by well-intentioned white people who are unaware of the hidden messages being sent to them" (DeAngelis, 2009, para. 4). This definition can be expanded to include similar phrases that target or seek to characterize any particular racial, ethnic, religious, or other group. Microaggressions may sound less serious because of their name, but they can be just as harmful to team members over time as more apparent forms of discrimination. Because you might not even realize you've just committed a microaggression, you may not know there's any behavior you need to correct unless someone brings it to your attention. If they do, your initial reaction may be to protest. Just like with unconscious biases, you may not have meant your comment to be harmful, and you may not think of yourself as racist or sexist, but that doesn't mean that there's no way you could ever say something racist or sexist, or that your comment wasn't harmful.

Worse, people who experience microaggressions are often expected to suffer them in silence, since the amount of harm being done is less obvious. They may be accused of being "too sensitive" if they complain about a microaggression they experienced, which can cause other members of the group to get upset with them and feel like they're making a big deal out of nothing. Of course, microaggressions cause very real harm, and they can be incredibly stressful and frustrating to people who experience them. This frustration is only multiplied when people feel like no one is on their side as they try to point out the unfairness of their situation. Part of creating an inclusive working space for everyone is taking microaggressions seriously and working to correct them when they occur. If you ignore them, you encourage your team members to see them as no big deal, and you can make the situation worse for those who are targeted.

To fully understand microaggressions, we'll start by looking at some common examples, some of which you may have experienced yourself without even knowing the words to describe them. Then we'll shift our attention to the most effective strategies for helping everyone understand how microaggressions harm others and what people can do to extract them from their vocabulary.

Examples of Microaggressions

In order to spot a microaggression, you must first know what you're looking for. In general, most microaggressions are phrases that may seem neutral or even positive on the surface, but which carry deeper meanings that completely change their tone for the recipient. Many of them have historical or cultural contexts that can shape how they sound to people within different racial or social groups. They can function like coded messages, where only some people are able to pick up on them and others may shrug them off without a second thought, including those who unthinkingly say them.

In many cases, it is better to say nothing at all than to say something which could be construed as harmful. Many microaggressions are knee-jerk reactions to certain observations that don't actually need to be said aloud. Being more conscious about what you say and relying on your mental filter will help you decide what contributes to a conversation or clarifies an issue and what can be left out entirely. Keep conversation appropriate for work, and listen for some of these common examples of microaggressions that could be making your team members uncomfortable.

"She's Crazy"

The word "crazy" is often thrown around with little care for its actual meaning or how it can impact people. Colloquially, "crazy" is often used to mean strange, unusual, intense, odd, or aggressive. It has become a catch-all word that can have a number of different interpretations depending on the situation. Someone might shake their head and say, "You're crazy!" when they see unusual behavior, or they might tell their coworker "Our boss is crazy" when they get assigned extra work. Even though the word has become so divorced from its original meaning, it still holds power, and it's important to recognize what the word really means and how it has been weaponized against people for decades.

Crazy, when taken literally, refers to mental illness. It paints people suffering from conditions like psychosis, schizophrenia, and bipolar disorder in a negative light, defining them only by their condition and not by their whole personality. Using the word "crazy" to refer to negative things in a general sense reinforces equally negative stigmas about people suffering from poor mental health and mental illnesses. If crazy is bad, then people who are "crazy" must be bad too.

Using "crazy" to refer to women in particular reinforces stereotypes of women being overcome by their emotions and therefore being less capable of self-control and clear thought than men. It invites comparisons to claims of "female hysteria" that once permeated the mental health field and which were almost always used as tools for the persecution of women. Rather than examining the situation women were living in, the stressors in their lives, and specific factors that might be contributing to mental illness, doctors would simply diagnose women with hysteria and send them to get some rest. As a result, mental health conditions went overlooked and the results of consistent prejudice and inequality on women's minds were ignored. Other examples of "crazy" as a vehicle for thinly-veiled sexism include the phrase "crazy ex-girlfriend" and the implication that if a woman seems to be acting "crazy," it must be "her time of the month." Either term only serves to belittle the feelings of women. These assumptions are harmful and can make women feel mistreated and like they're not being taken seriously.

Rather than continuing to use the word "crazy," encourage people to use more specific terms. Rather than calling their boss crazy, maybe they mean to say she is being unreasonable or unfair. Using more specific terminology comes with the added benefit of facilitating conversations. There's little to do about a "crazy" boss other than complain, but a team member can talk to you about a potential solution for being expected to perform unreasonable tasks. The clearer everyone's language is, the more productive the whole team can be.

"That's So Gay"

The phrase "that's so gay" is more common in younger demographics, but it can pervade older spaces too. It's typically used to express disappointment or disgust with something. It may seem like a harmless phrase, but it's actually far from it.

Calling something "gay" casts the same negative light on LGBT employees as "crazy" does for people with mental health issues. By equating gay with bad or weak, the phrase implies that these are qualities shared by gay people as well. Even if that's not the intended meaning, LGBT employees could feel like they're being persecuted or put down every time they hear it. The workplace becomes hostile to them, all because of a small phrase that could easily and painlessly be replaced.

This is another circumstance where more specific language is the best solution. Rather than saying something is "gay," encourage people to say it's unfortunate, disappointing, or frustrating. Cut to the heart of the issue so you can come up with a real solution to the problem at hand.

"You're So Articulate"

"You're so articulate" is usually said by white people who are speaking to people of color, especially black people. Many people who use it intend it as a compliment. They're trying to say they're impressed with how the other person speaks, but this begs the question, what did they expect? Most people who comment on how "articulate" someone is are operating on the assumption that all black people speak with African-American Vernacular English (AAVE), slur or drawl their speech, or otherwise speak in a way that some people might perceive as uneducated. Additionally, it suggests that the use of AAVE is unprofessional, equating it to being inarticulate and implying that there's something wrong with speaking in a stereotypically non-white way. In other words, the phrase "you're so articulate" follows the logic that black people as a whole aren't as intelligent as white people and that differences in speech that more closely replicate how white people speak are a marker of intelligence. It should be plain to see why this is taken as offensive by so many black people.

These kinds of phrases can be hard to work out of white peoples' vocabularies because they're usually intended as compliments, even though they really function as an insult to someone's race and culture. However, understanding the implications of the phrase can help people recognize why it's hurtful and help them stop saying it. There's no need to replace the phrase; by working to undermine the beliefs that speech patterns equate to intelligence and that people of color are less intelligent than white people, there will no longer be any reason to compliment how articulate anyone sounds. Instead, if people are looking for a better compliment that makes everyone feel good, they can try complimenting the actual content of what someone is saying rather than the way they say it.

"I Couldn't Tell You Were Trans"

Many workplaces have transgender employees, and just as many have people who don't routinely interact with transgender people. Because of this, they may be unaware that saying things like "I had no idea you were trans" isn't the compliment they mean it to be. The intended meaning is that the trans person looks good, but the implication hidden under the words is that the person giving the compliment is scrutinizing their appearance, trying to look for tells that would tip them off to the person being trans. This is uncomfortable, as it's a level of scrutiny that cisgender people, those whose gender identity matches what they were assigned at birth, are rarely if ever subjected to. You would never tell a cisgender woman that she "looks exactly like a woman," since it carries the message that she's not a real woman, and yet many people say the same thing to trans women and expect it to be taken as a compliment.

These kinds of statements also imply that the transgender person is expected to conform to their expectations of how people who are male, female, or nonbinary must look. This reinforces some of the potentially harmful gender stereotypes discussed in Chapter 7. Finally, some discomfort comes from the assumption that a trans person's ability to make their physical appearance match their gender is the most important thing to them, when they'd likely be more interested in being recognized for their contributions at the office. Rather than praising someone's appearance, whether they're cis or trans, consider emphasizing the value of their work and recognizing the efforts they're making to support the team.

"Where Are You Really From?"

This microaggression is commonly directed toward people of different ethnicities, especially those who may have physical features that make them look somewhat racially ambiguous. Typically, person A will ask person B where they're from, usually expecting person B to be from a different country or region. If person B replies that they're from somewhere nearby, person A might ask, "No, where are you *really* from?" The implication in their repeated question is that person B wasn't actually born in the country. Alternatively, they might ask, "Where are your parents from?" believing person B's parents to be first-generation immigrants.

This is a frustrating question for a number of different reasons. For one, it disregards the wide variety of races and ethnicities who live within North America. There is an implicit othering in the question, suggesting that someone isn't *really* from here, which is untrue regardless of whether they've lived in North America for just a few years or their whole lives. Additionally, the question is invasive. It's a demand for information, not simple small talk, as evidenced by the initial brush-off answer not being accepted. Someone may not want to talk about their family history for any number of reasons, or they may prefer to bring that information up voluntarily rather than feel like they're being put on the spot and must answer the question right away. Depending on how often someone is asked this sort of question, it can be exhausting as well. It may not seem like it from an outsider's perspective, but imagine if you were living in a foreign country and you constantly had people asking where you were from. It can understandably get old fast.

Some people are perfectly happy to speak about their family's origins and their cultural backgrounds, while others would prefer not to feel like they're required to answer these kinds of questions. Just as it might be rude to ask about other personal information, like their political party or how much money they make, if they don't bring these topics up themselves, treating someone's ethnicity as a subject for small talk is a tiresome and often frustrating practice and a poor way to practice inclusivity. Instead, create environments where people feel comfortable speaking about themselves to the extent that they want to share, and don't push for answers that someone doesn't want to give. If you're just looking to chit-chat, pick a more neutral topic like the weather or sports.

"I Don't See Color"

Many people may have every intention of trying to take a more inclusive stance in their lives, but the phrase "I don't see color" isn't the way to do it. On the surface, it may sound like a progressive, diversity-friendly stance. After all, if you don't see color, you aren't acting with prejudice toward any particular race, right? However, this microaggression unfortunately ignores the very real cultural differences between people of different races. Consider why you're investing in diversity efforts in the first place, if not to bring people of differing backgrounds and cultures together and to benefit from their differences. The phrase "I don't see color" ignores that differences between people of different racial groups are a good thing, instead lumping everyone into the same category. If you're trying to lead your organization toward being more inclusive and eliminating racial bias, you'll have a hard time doing so if you pretend race itself doesn't exist.

This microaggression also fails to account for the differences that could spark disagreements within the group, such as differing values. If you don't take the time to learn and respect everyone's cultural practices, you may have a harder time mediating conflicts and coming up with compromises. It's also worth considering exactly what you might mean when you say you don't see color. If everyone is the same race in your eyes, it's unlikely that you're saying you see yourself as black—instead, you're probably saying you see everyone as white, which introduces issues of ethnocentrism. Seeing everyone through your lens rather than respecting that people from different backgrounds have equally different practices is, in a sense, imposing your culture on others and expecting them to conform to it. It is closer to assimilation than it is to true diversity and inclusion.

Additionally, this phrase disregards differences in lived experiences that are a product of systemic racism. While there is still inequality, there are always going to be experiences that people of color have which white people will never personally experience. For example, most white people are able to grow up being taught that the cops will protect them, and they should always call the police if they feel threatened. On the other hand, people of color are generally more wary to call on the police for help.

This is due to instances of racial bias and profiling that can and often do escalate the use of force against black Americans, with one study finding that black men "are about 2.5 times more likely to be killed by police" than white men in the U.S. (Edwards, Lee, & Esposito, 2019, para. 13). Racial bias in policing is an issue in other parts of North America like Canada as well. This is an experience that is fundamentally different from the way white people interact with the police, and it is just one example of the ways in which the "I don't see color" rhetoric glosses over existing problems for people of color without fixing them in any meaningful way.

Rather than striving not to see color, it's a better practice to recognize the unique challenges and experiences of people of color and account for them in your policies and actions. Understand how systemic racism can and does harm people, and bring these issues to light so you can address them rather than ignoring their existence.

How to Deal with Microaggressions

Many companies and organizations fail to address microaggressions at all. They may not recognize the real harm these kinds of phrases cause, or they may decide they are unwilling to get involved in conversations employees have with each other. However, a failure to act is almost as bad as encouraging this kind of behavior. In a way, organizations that allow microaggressions to continue are endorsing them and writing off concerns that they make the group a more hostile and uncomfortable place for many team members. Recognizing that microaggressions exist and negatively impact many people is the first step in dealing with them appropriately and effectively.

Those who do attempt to correct microaggressions often fall somewhat short of their goals. To many people, trying to correct microaggressions can feel like policing their language, especially if they fail to see the harm in many of their statements. This makes it very difficult to convince people on the team who aren't affected by microaggressions that they're worth the effort and energy used to educate the team and correct these behaviors. If you go about the process in the wrong way, you may only reinforce their beliefs that this is a pointless or even harmful endeavor.

An effective strategy for eliminating microaggressions without making anyone feel like they're being treated unfairly involves recognizing that microaggressions have power, being clear and straightforward about how these words can hurt, and working together with everyone to develop a strategy or taskforce for addressing these kinds of issues.

Take Them Seriously

The first and most obvious step for dealing with microaggressions is to treat them as seriously as they deserve to be treated. If you act like microaggressions are unimportant and don't cause as much harm as other types of prejudice, this attitude will rub off on everyone else, and they won't be as committed to removing them from their vocabulary. When everyone understands that their words are causing harm, even if it's entirely inadvertently, they're more likely to try to correct the behavior.

Of course, if you simply say "don't say that, it's hurtful," you're not going to convince many people that they've said something worthy of criticism. Many people only continue to use microaggressions because they don't understand how they can make others feel alienated and isolated. In fact, many microaggressions come off as progressive statements on the surface, though reading into their implications paints a much grimmer story. Once you've established that you're not going to tolerate microaggressions and started to show everyone why these phrases and attitudes don't have a place within your team, reinforce this by explaining why each phrase is harmful.

Explain Why a Phrase Is Harmful

Even if someone is willing to accept that something, they said could have been taken the wrong way, they may not be ready to agree that the phrase itself was harmful. For this, you may need to teach them more about the origin of phrases rooted in racism, or about the deeper implications that make microaggressions unacceptable. The breakdowns of the examples listed earlier in this chapter include the reasoning behind why people find these phrases offensive and upsetting. Refer back to these when explaining them to team members who may be using them. If you encounter a microaggression that's not on the above list, do some research to better understand why it can be hurtful before having a discussion with your employee.

Explaining the problems of each phrase can help push back against claims of censorship and "reverse racism" as well. Microaggressions shouldn't be part of the workplace, not because they are arbitrarily defined and restricted or because you're trying to act as the "thought police," but because they're not appropriate to express in a professional setting due to their discriminatory nature. Microaggressions are far from the only things that aren't appropriate for work. Employees and group members for most organizations are barred from using other inappropriate language like cursing or sexually explicit words and innuendos for much the same reason that microaggressions shouldn't be allowed, which is that they can make people uncomfortable and aren't suitable for the environment.

After clarifying your stance on microaggressions and starting to teach people why they matter, you can work on developing a team or specific strategy for spreading and reinforcing this message.

Work with Your Team to Develop a Comprehensive Education Strategy

Rather than judging every instance of microaggression on a case-by-case basis, or ignoring microaggressions altogether until they become a problem, create a clear strategy for educating the whole team about the dangers of microaggressions. You can go about this in a few different ways. You might hold a presentation to raise awareness of microaggressions, explaining what they are and why they can upset people. You could put up posters around the office reminding people of their danger. You could create a task force dedicated to addressing this problem, or ensure everyone gets training that includes lessons on microaggressions.

Whatever strategy you choose, make sure to involve everyone. Get people to help out by making posters or pitching ideas for training sessions. Ask for feedback and invite people to speak up if they feel some information is off or if it targets anyone unfairly. When all team members are involved in creating and upholding diversity policies, they're more likely to be followed, and the whole experience will feel more inclusive.

Chapter 9: How Personal Bias Becomes Systemic Bias in the Workplace

Not all bias comes from the same source, nor is it perpetuated in the same ways. We have already looked at the difference between unconscious and conscious bias, but in the context of previous conversations, they have mainly been explored on the individual, or personal, level. In other words, we looked at bias as the failing of a single person. While there can certainly be biases held by just one member of a team, a much more insidious form of bias arises in a more systemic form.

It's very tempting to think of incidents of discrimination in the workplace or group as the result of a "bad apple." This sort of framing makes the idea of stamping out racism and other prejudices in a company sound much easier. You only have to deal with one person, whom you can handle by either showing them the error of their ways or, if the situation is dire enough, removing them from the team. However, the focus on personal bias ignores the many ways in which bias pervades our societal norms, our cultural assumptions, and some of the policies we take for granted.

Systemic bias within a society often leads to individuals sharing these biases. You are raised in a society that endorses viewing a particular race, religion, or cultural group as superior to others in order to, consciously or unconsciously, perpetuate inequality. Therefore, it's possible some of these biases might become rooted in your brain since you've been taught to accept them as true for so long. Gender roles, which we discussed in Chapter 7, are a type of systemic bias that frequently disadvantages women by defining what they are and are not expected to do. Since there are biases in the way laws are written, the conversations you have with others, and media and pop culture, your subconscious picks up on these ideas of how women should behave and eventually internalizes them, whether they're true or not.

Just as systemic bias can lead to personal bias, so too can personal bias create systemic bias within an organization. If you or other members of upper-level management in your group or workplace have unconscious biases, you might unthinkingly write company policies and protocols in accordance with these biases. For example, you might choose to limit your talent search to potential new hires who can meet with you during weekdays because you see this as more professional, not realizing that such a policy would immediately disadvantage anyone who can't take time off from their current job or who would struggle to find childcare during that time. This is just one example out of many possibilities, but it shows how personal bias can find its way into structural policies, affecting the whole company.

A solid grasp of systemic bias and what it means for your company will help you become better at recognizing it and rooting it out, supporting your continued efforts to create an inclusive workplace.

What Is Systemic Bias?

Systemic bias also goes by the name "institutional bias." It refers to types of bias that are ingrained within the laws, social mores, and common practices of a society. In a more general sense, it can be viewed as a preference for a certain method for completing a task or process that tends to result in a particular outcome. Systemic bias is typically deeply rooted within a company and the society the company is a part of. These pervasive biases are typically very difficult to eliminate compared to other forms, as they become normalized, accepted, and frequently looked over by those who aren't personally affected by it.

Systemic bias is often the product of legislation meant to criminalize a particular group. For example, drug laws, specifically those heavily criminalizing marijuana during U.S. President Richard Nixon's "war on drugs," tend to disproportionately harm black communities. According to the domestic policy chief at the time, John Ehrlichman, many of these laws were targeted toward antiwar protestors and black people, neither of whom polled well with Nixon. Ehrlichman recounts, "by getting the public to associate the hippies with marijuana and [black people] with heroin, and then criminalizing both heavily, we could disrupt those communities" (LoBianco, 2016, para. 3). These laws created and enabled some of the systemic racism issues inherent in drug policies and policing that exist to this day, and they contribute to the harmful idea that black people are somehow naturally more likely to do drugs, as well as their recreational drug use making them "lazy" or otherwise unfit for work. These are harmful stereotypes that get perpetuated by biases in the criminal justice system. They lead to higher rates of arrest for drug-related crimes in black communities, with black people "arrested for violating marijuana possession laws at nearly four times the rates of whites" despite the fact that "both ethnicities consume marijuana at roughly the same rates" (National Organization for the Reform of Marijuana Laws, 2020, para. 1). Many of the commonly-held associations between minority groups and drug use are largely the result of systemic racism and bias in making arrests, rather than the real statistics.

How does this affect your business? While you may not be the one responsible for writing your country, state, or province's drug laws, they still affect who you hire and keep around at your company. If someone has a criminal record, even if it's only for possession of a small amount of marijuana, you may be less likely to hire them compared to someone with a clean record. Given that black people are so much more likely to be arrested and face harsher punishments for drug use, despite the rates of marijuana use between black and white people being about equal, this could put black applicants at an unfair disadvantage compared to white ones who may have committed the same offenses and simply been under less scrutiny. You almost certainly aren't going into the hiring process purposefully looking to hire more white people, but if you don't account for differences in how society treats black drug offenders in comparison to white ones, you just might end up doing so anyway.

The above example showcases the bias pipeline at work. A systemic issue in the larger society is internalized by the society's members and converted to a personal one held by individuals in administrative positions. Then it is converted back to being systemic on a smaller scale, within the company. When systemic biases that can result in unequal pay, unfair hiring processes, and preferential treatment within the workplace go unchecked, they can create widescale discrimination that goes far beyond the harm of a single person's prejudices, all without being apparent to those who hold these biases.

Include Systemic Bias Awareness in Unconscious Bias Training

Unconscious bias recognition training is important for all companies, but that's not where the bias discussion should end. It's important to also recognize that many of these unconscious biases don't operate on an individual level, but on a systemic one. Bias that manifests in company policies and perceptions held by the whole group can be especially damaging. Including an explanation of systemic bias in your unconscious bias training helps everyone call out these policies when they see them. It also tells people who are negatively impacted by systemic bias that they are not fighting alone. While it may take some time to overhaul the traditional way of doing things in favor of new systems that contain less implicit bias, employees will know you're on their side every step of the way, and that you are capable of recognizing that less obvious forms of bias can make the workplace more hostile for some people.

When creating presentations or other types of training about systemic bias, be sure to use examples to introduce the dangers of systemic bias to employees who might not have ever heard about it before. Select examples that are relevant to your company's operation or hiring concerns on a more general level. As an example, a bias known as the network gap makes it easier for people who already have a foothold in a given industry to progress their career and climb up the corporate ladder. In other words, this bias is the manifestation of the phrase, "It's not what you know, but who you know." The network gap can make it harder for those without the right professional connections to find well-paying work in their field, which often puts people in minority groups at a significant disadvantage as they may not have all the same opportunities to network.

Given that many companies are still under pressure to hire more diverse workforces, the network gap makes certain industries very insular. This can in turn influence discrimination in the hiring process, as good candidates are passed over in favor of those who have more connections. Other important manifestations of systemic bias to mention are certain dress codes that unfairly target an ethnicity or religious group, the aforementioned like-me bias, and white privilege, which will be discussed in greater detail in Chapter 10.

Your Influence as a Leader

As the leader of your organization, you hold the brunt of the responsibility for ensuring personal biases do not become structural ones. You decide which policies to implement, which means any biases you might hold can easily become systemic ones that permeate the entire company. In the interest of preventing this, educating yourself on biases like those mentioned previously is key. The better you understand how bias can affect you, the better you will be at stamping it out.

Additionally, it helps to be open to change. It's tempting to continue to use old systems because they worked in the past, but many of these old systems haven't been revisited to account for diversity and inclusion, and as a result they suffer from the results of systemic bias. Just because something has been around for a long time doesn't mean it's the best option—in fact, when it comes to diversity, typically the opposite is true. Wage gaps for women and people of color have been a consistent issue of payroll discrimination for decades. It is a familiar result of bias, but it shouldn't be allowed to continue if there's something you can do to fix it. Rather than uncritically relying on traditional methods that might cause harm to some members of your team, recognize that change is a part of growth, and that you won't be able to create an inclusive workplace unless you embrace the necessity of change.

As a leader, you have the power to show your employees how they should be acting. Your actions set the tone for the entire company. If you treat prejudice seriously and frequently test for the presence of systemic bias in different policies, the rest of your team will be on the lookout for them too. If you demonstrate that you have a zero-tolerance policy for bias, everyone will know just how important a consideration it is. If you're not just tolerant of but actively excited about the prospect of change and improvement, your employees will be as well. Set a positive tone that prioritizes inclusivity while keeping a careful eye out for bias so you don't accidentally introduce it into your company.

Teaching Others How to React

Consider this scenario: one of your employees points out that a policy you've been using in your company for years is biased against some team members.

Maybe your company has a dress code policy that forbids hats and head coverings in the building, which could be used to unfairly target people wearing them for religious reasons. You have two options in responding to this. You could shrug, throw your hands up, and decide that rules are rules and everyone has to follow them, or you could adjust the rule to be more inclusive.

Think of how either option looks to people who are affected by these biases. In the first option, you come off as uncaring about their issues. You don't do anything to fix the problem, instead deciding it's not your fault and you're more concerned about appearing preferential by adjusting the rule than you are about actually eliminating inequalities. In the second, your actions tell them you care about the prejudices these employees may be facing and you're on their side. You show you are proactive and that you value their religion and culture. Additionally, think of the message your actions communicate to employees who aren't part of the marginalized group. If they see that you are unconcerned with the harmful results of the rule, they'll be unconcerned too, and more likely to believe they can get away with other prejudiced behaviors. If they see you take it seriously, they'll know that discriminatory actions and policies, even those that are accidental, are not allowed under any circumstances.

Creating a more inclusive working space means involving everyone in the changes you're implementing. By leading through positive example, you show everyone who works for you what the expected response to issues of inequality should be, and they will follow your lead.

Avoid Holding Up Outdated Systems Based on Prejudice

Resistance to change is one of the biggest problems affecting leaders and management teams, not just with regards to inclusivity but in every aspect of the company. There are many parts of workflow that could be improved if making these changes wasn't seen as such a terrifying prospect. Change is inherently uncertain, and you may have many reservations about how the new system will work out and whether or not it will improve anything. But if you never try new methods, you'll never know if you could have significantly improved productivity and quality of life at the company.

Take the example of digitizing files that you previously stored as physical copies. This is a huge space-saver, and it generally saves time too, as people can search an online database for the information they need rather than having to pull it from the filing cabinet. You also don't have to be physically near the files to access them. This is an example of a change that many companies were initially reluctant to make but that most have made by now in our highly digital age. It's also one that has been entirely revolutionary for productivity and efficiency. If you are resistant to change in all areas, you miss out on many opportunities to improve.

Committing to changing outdated, harmful policies is similarly important. You may be reluctant to change the way you've always done the hiring process, or to alter how you complete payroll, but these changes are good and necessary for being an equitable leader. If there is a system within your company that only exists because of prejudice, or which has been misused to discriminate against people, changing it is the only real option for improving everyone's experiences. When you replace these with new policies, you just might find that the new methods work much better after all.

Chapter 10: Understanding Privilege

A great deal of inequality within organizations occurs without any purposeful attempt to harm others. We've seen this with concepts like unconscious bias and microaggressions, which do not intentionally discriminate against anyone and yet can be used in a discriminatory way. Oftentimes, these harmful systems are perpetuated for months or years without proper recognition of their issues, because their effect is invisible to the people in charge who aren't impacted by them. It frequently takes someone who is affected by policies founded in prejudice speaking up in order to get these issues corrected at all. This isn't the result of malice on your part as a leader, but rather the unfortunate by-product of a disparity in privilege.

Privilege is a type of inequality that typically involves one group having more opportunities and advantages than another group. The most common example is white privilege, which refers to the tendency for many white people to receive preferential treatment that people of color don't have access to. This of course doesn't mean that if you are white, you are guaranteed to have an easy life, nor does it mean that you will have a terrible life filled with struggle just because you are black. Instead, it simply means that not everyone starts out on an equal playing field. You can see similar factors at play when you look at class differences. Someone who is born into a rich family might have more privileges because their family could afford to send them to a private school with better education, or pay for private tutoring, which leads to them getting higher grades and acing their aptitude tests. This in turn means they can get into competitive colleges with top-rated programs, which looks better on a resume than someone who may be equally smart, but who didn't have as many opportunities and had to settle for an education at a cheaper, less well-renowned college.

Additionally, when a family doesn't have to worry about issues that affect people in poverty, like food insecurity, and the stresses that come with financial trouble, they don't have to do things like work a second job and sacrifice family time, which can put kids raised within these households at an advantage compared to their peers. Again, there may be specific personal conditions and unfortunate circumstances that people who live more privileged lives still have to endure, but in general their privileges make it easier for them to achieve professional and financial success.

Privilege can become a problem within organizations because it is often difficult to detect. People may not recognize systems that give an advantage to one group of people over another because they are on the advantaged side and therefore don't have the personal experience to recognize how these systems can cause harm. Many people might get angry at the idea that they have privileges not afforded to others because they have had difficult lives, misunderstanding the real meaning of the sentiment. All of these factors increase the likelihood that without listening to people who don't get to enjoy the same privileges, the inequality will remain unquestioned, and some team members will remain at a disadvantage.

How Privilege Goes Unchecked

Privilege is almost always unrecognized if you don't make a purposeful effort to consider it in your decisions. By its nature, privilege is something that is taken for granted. Those whom it negatively affects may recognize it, but those who experience it rarely do if they haven't been trained to look out for it.

This is one of the many reasons why efforts to improve diversity and inclusion are so important. With a greater commitment to inclusion, it is easier to spot inequalities. You'll also be able to educate yourself about privileges that you may enjoy that other people don't have access to, as well as any privileges others have but you don't. It's especially easy for inequalities born of privilege to fly under the radar because many of them are the result of systemic issues, either within the company or within the greater society. Now that you have learned about the dangers of unconscious bias and systemic inequalities, you are better equipped to recognize your privileges and how they might color your view of a situation.

There is power in point of view. Privilege is easy to take for granted because we all have limited points of view. When we look at a situation, we look at it through the lens of our own experiences. For example, if you graduated from college and got your degree, you probably thought about all the hard work you put in to get there. If someone suggests that people in minority groups don't always have the same access to education and therefore they have a disadvantage when it comes to graduating from prestigious colleges, you might be tempted to argue that it's untrue, and instead suggest that the inequality only represents a difference in how hard the two of you worked. However, is this really true? You might have put a significant amount of effort into studying and completing homework assignments, yes, but just because someone doesn't get to attend college doesn't mean they don't put effort into other areas of their lives. They may even have to work two jobs or take double shifts at lower-paying jobs to make half as much as someone who lands a high-paying job thanks to their degree. "Working hard" isn't the only factor at play here, but it's not always easy to see that if you haven't directly experienced systematic inequality yourself.

Some privileges are almost invisible to the people who have them. For example, let's say you work on the second floor of a building with no elevator. This might not be a problem for you if you can simply take the stairs. Sure, it might be a minor inconvenience if you're carrying something heavy, but you don't need elevator accessibility to get around. Now consider the same situation from the perspective of someone with a disability that restricts their mobility. Now, suddenly, the stairs become a significant issue. People who use wheelchairs wouldn't be able to access the office at all, and people with other mobility-related conditions might have to spend much more time climbing them. Despite the clear inequality that not providing an elevator creates, there are still plenty of buildings without them because the people who built them were privileged enough not to need them. Their privilege allowed them to forget about or ignore the people whom they were putting at a disadvantage.

Issues of privilege within a company can manifest in exactly the same way. A lack of perspective on certain issues can keep you from recognizing a problem that is all too apparent to others. This is why having diversity in the workplace and within different groups is so important. A person who grew up in poverty could tell you that hiring people based on what school they could afford to attend rather than on their own merits gives an advantage to wealthier job applicants. A person with a disability could immediately identify the issues with a building that's not accessible to everyone. Even if these are problems you might not pick up on yourself, the more diverse your team is, the more likely it is that someone will pick up on these instances of inequality and point them out so they can be corrected.

Unlearning Misconceptions About Privilege

Now that you have a good grasp on what privilege is and how it can become a problem for your team if left unchecked, you can start taking steps to acknowledge the role it plays within your organization and correct these disparities. That being said, even though you know how important it is to account for, you may still have difficulties fully accepting the role privilege has played in stacking the deck in your favor, in a manner of speaking. It's not always easy to understand this, in part due to your own limited experience with systemic prejudice, but also because of the many misconceptions that make it harder to talk about privilege.

Many people reject the idea of talking about privilege at all, let alone correcting it, because they feel it persecutes them unfairly for factors outside of their control. They may believe that the terms used to discuss privilege are racist or "reverse racist." They may also feel like they are being asked to feel guilty about their privilege, when this is far from the truth. Some people are reluctant to talk about these issues because they don't feel it is their place, even though the best way to roll out inclusive policies is to involve people from different backgrounds. Alternatively, they may think that privilege only exists in relation to race, when in reality it can affect many different groups of people. Addressing these misconceptions can be a huge help in opening people up to the idea of having productive conversations about privilege and fostering real change.

"I Can't Have Privilege Because I Have Faced Hardships in My Life"

This is the most common response to learning about privilege, and it's not hard to see why. For most people who are not familiar with the term in this context, hearing "privilege" makes them think of people who grew up in mansions and had their every need catered to by their waitstaff. Therefore, it becomes easy to reject the idea that they could also benefit from privilege, as they have faced many of the same ups and downs of life as everyone else. Since they're not as privileged as the richest people, and since they have been through difficult moments in their lives, they conclude that they can't possibly be privileged.

It's easy to sympathize with this point of view at first glance. If someone tells you you're more privileged, it can feel more like an attack than a statement of fact. If hard work is highly valued, then the idea that you have been coasting through your life without putting in as much work as others comes off as an especially grave insult. You may feel that it seeks to invalidate all of the struggles you have experienced up to this moment, suggesting that these difficulties were inherently less devastating. It may even come off like you are being told to quit being sad about your problems because "other people have it worse," which can understandably undermine your confidence in the idea of privilege as a whole.

This line of thinking points to a fundamental misunderstanding of what privilege means. When we talk about privilege on the societal or company level, we're not talking about the day-to-day difficulties that people face. Even the richest person on the planet is going to have some moments where they feel angry or upset, but this doesn't mean they don't still have privilege. Rather than pointing to the specific good and bad experiences people have been through in their lives, the privileges in question are those that are deeply entrenched in social norms, public perceptions, and systemic biases. The fact that you have experienced financial hardships or put in hard work to get where you are today can coexist with the notion that in some ways your life has also been affected by privilege. There are opportunities that you experience which others never get the chance to enjoy due to structural and systemic inequalities. These are the issues that recognizing privilege seeks to address, not individual moments of struggle.

A great deal of systemic bias can come from the rewriting of narratives about people in minority groups. Most people who are white and straight have the privilege of seeing themselves in many heroic figures, both real and fictional. There are notable heroes who look like them and share their culture and values, and their perspective on historical events is taught in most schools. This is doubly true for men. In many ways, people in these demographics are viewed as the default, and every other race, sexuality, and gender is seen as a deviation from the norm. There is less representation for women and people of color. The representation that exists for people with disabilities is incredibly limited and often plagued with stereotypes and harmful language. People who are part of religious minority groups may only see representations of themselves in media as offensive caricatures, with few real representations of their lives and their cultures. Minority groups by and large are not given the spotlight in the history books either. Their contributions are frequently ignored altogether, and the discrimination they face is routinely downplayed or conveniently left out. For example, many Native American and Indigenous populations were driven out of their homes and killed in conflicts with European settlers, yet history books frequently focus on the bravery of explorers like Christopher Columbus for "discovering" a continent that was already populated. This is just one of the many ways in which privilege and education commingle, and it assists in conditioning you to turn a blind eye to inequalities you may not have even realized existed.

Even though an individual white, straight male might live through difficult life events or face discrimination on other axes like disabilities or mental health issues, this doesn't invalidate their other privileges. They still get to see themselves painted as heroes in the history books and on TV. They still have role models to look up to. In short, privilege does not become nonexistent just because other hardships occur. Accepting this goes a long way toward rejecting the idea that someone pointing out your privilege is meant to be a personal attack. It is an observation, not a moral judgment.

"Only Those Who Lack Privileges Should Talk About Them"

As previously discussed, people who have privileges often have a harder time recognizing their impact. However, this doesn't mean they should be excluded from conversations entirely. In fact, this can have the undesirable effect of placing the majority of the work of accounting for differences in privilege on those who have been most affected by it. It's true that it may take some time to fully grasp the idea of privileges and to be informed enough to make a difference, but by educating yourself about these issues you can become just as committed to accounting for bias as anyone who has directly experienced it.

Additionally, there's a good chance you have experienced a lack of privilege at some point in your life or another. If you're white, you may not have been disadvantaged because of your race, but you could have been treated unfairly based on other factors like your class, appearance, and physical health. Think of the way it made you feel when you watched others easily accomplish something you struggled at, not because they worked harder, but because they were naturally more talented or they had an advantage over you that was outside of your reach. You probably thought it was unfair. You likely thought someone should do something to make the situation less biased toward certain types of people, and it's possible you took action to incite this change yourself. Keep this in mind when someone comes to you about a situation of discrimination within your organization, and let it fuel your desire to correct the injustice.

"The Term 'White Privilege' Is Racist"

The mere act of discussing privilege at all may be misconstrued as racist. This is especially true with the phrase "white privilege," which has become the type of privilege that is most familiar to people, even if they don't fully understand what it means. It's understandable why some might think that suggesting all white people have privilege could be seen as racist. Some could even say the term is used purposefully to make white people feel bad about being white. It often comes up in discussions of "reverse racism," which is the idea that programs meant to address discrimination and a lack of diversity like affirmative action are actually a form of racism against white people. Racism is directed toward minority groups, while reverse racism is theoretically directed toward majority groups in the population.

While the "reverse racism" narrative can be tempting to believe for people who feel like their jobs are threatened by more diverse hiring measures, it simply doesn't hold much water, or at least not within North America. For one, reverse racism lacks the historical, structural and systemic inequalities that make racism so harmful to people in minority groups. Diversity measures are meant to make up for a lack of non-white job candidates and group members, and few, if any, actually require that there be more people of color than white people in an organization. There can be unfair stereotypes and assumptions made about white people, but these are born of individual prejudices rather than widespread inequality. These prejudices also lack the power imbalance that is characteristic of racism. The Alberta Civil Liberties Research Centre points out that "While expressions of racial prejudice directed at white people may hurt the white person/people individually or personally," they also "do not have the power or authority to affect the white person's social/economic/political location and privileges" (n.d., para. 2). In other words, there is no threat of the restriction or removal of rights explicit or implicit in prejudice directed toward white people. Therefore, while these words and actions can hurt and should be condemned just as firmly as racist remarks, they are not entrenched in the power imbalance that facilitates acts of discrimination.

Discussions of race and racial inequalities are not racist by nature, nor are the policies that seek to undo some of the damage caused by systemic racism in North America. They do not perpetuate reverse racism. Therefore, the act of pointing out white privilege is not one motivated by racist or even prejudiced sentiments, but instead one meant to improve inclusivity.

"Privilege Only Exists for White People"

This misconception is almost the polar opposite of the previous one. It suggests that white people are the only ones who are benefited by privileges, and therefore are the only ones who need to be conscious of how privilege plays a role in their lives. In practice, this idea is completely untrue. While white privilege does exist, this doesn't mean that white people can't be discriminated against for other reasons. Additionally, people can experience privilege based on much more than just the color of their skin.

Disparities in privilege can occur for various reasons. Earlier in this chapter, we looked at how ableism is perpetuated through the adherence to privileges for people without disabilities. There are many other examples. A straight and cisgender person may have more privileges than one from the LGBT community. In particular, marriage equality was a significant issue up until only a few years ago, and same-sex couples may still become targets of harassment as a result of prejudice. Those who have more money enjoy privileges like better access to healthcare, better education, and less finance-related stress. The vast majority of companies close their offices for Christmas, but very few close on holidays for other religions like Rosh Hashanah and Diwali, usually requiring employees to get pre-approval to take these days off. Each of these examples and many more can apply to people of color just as frequently as they apply to white people. There are black Christians, rich Asians, and straight Middle Eastern people who are disadvantaged by policies that affect one part of their identity while experiencing the privileges of another. Therefore, it is false to say that privilege is something only white people need to worry about. Privilege can apply to people of all races and affect many more aspects of someone's life.

"Accepting I Have Privilege Means Feeling Guilty"

When people hear they have privilege, they may get defensive—not because they don't think it's true on some level, but because they feel guilty about benefiting from it for so long without acknowledging it. Guilt is unpleasant, and it can lead people to firmly declare that privileges don't exist or that they aren't really affected by them so they can mitigate some of the guilt. Certain people may also be under the impression that by pointing out privilege, someone is expressly trying to make you feel guilty.

This is a misunderstanding of the reason why it's so important to talk about privilege. The goal is not to make people feel guilty about benefiting from a system that has put them first. Guilt isn't productive, and it won't help anyone rid the organization of harmful policies. The goal is to help people see that there is a problem so they can get on board with fixing it. There's no need to feel guilty about your privileges, so long as you recognize them and work to ensure everyone receives the same treatment you do. Learning about your privilege is an opportunity to grow and help other people, and treating it this way rather than encouraging anyone to feel bad about their privileges keeps the focus on the systemic issues that need to change rather than on the individual level.

Chapter 11: Why Is Race So Hard to Talk About?

To put it mildly, discussions about race can be uncomfortable. They involve confronting issues that you might otherwise not discuss, and they require you to be able to see things from someone else's point of view, which can often be a difficult task. Whether these discussions are happening within a single racial group or between people of different races, in a professional setting or as a casual chat, one thing is for certain: talking about race is tough.

Given that most people are reluctant to bring up race at all in conversation, it can be hard to normalize the idea of understanding and respecting the different experiences of white people and people of color. If you can't talk about someone's race, how can you explain why one person thinks a certain policy is fine and the other feels like it unfairly targets them due to its association with prejudices? It's not easy to bring up race in an honest and blunt way, which can lead to people tiptoeing around the issue. They might insist that the policy isn't harmful because of race-related reasons but because of other factors like the amount of work someone does, which can obscure the point of the discussion and insult the person who is being targeted by suggesting they don't work hard. Refusing to talk about race means that racial differences cannot be celebrated; instead, everyone must pretend as though they don't exist.

Many people would prefer to not recognize race at all, instead claiming they're "colorblind" or using the fact that race doesn't really exist biologically as a reason to disregard it entirely. While race itself is a social construct, that doesn't mean that it doesn't have a real, significant impact on how you interact with society. Other people might make judgments about you based on the color of your skin, positive or negative. You may have been taught to approach a certain problem one way, while people from other races have an entirely different problem-solving method for the same issue. Given that racism is very real and still present in many institutions, it colors the way people from different races are taught to interact with authority figures like police officers and management. All of these differences are real and need to be accounted for, and they can't be if you and your team are afraid to have serious conversations about the role race plays in people's lives.

As a leader in diversity and inclusion, you should be committed to making everyone feel comfortable when talking about race. This means creating an environment where no one feels persecuted because of how they look or their culture. It also means creating an environment free from blame and guilt, focusing on possible solutions rather than getting caught up in punishments and shame. Even though these conversations may be uncomfortable at first, they are necessary to ensure no one on your team is silently struggling. The more you have these kinds of discussions, the easier and more casual they will become, and the better team members of different races will come to understand each other's' experiences. Yes, race is hard to talk about, but that doesn't have to keep you from doing it anyway.

Why Discussing Race Creates Discomfort

Despite best efforts to the contrary, there is a tendency to see race primarily as something negative. After all, many people face discrimination because of their race. If we were all one race, indistinguishable from each other, some people argue, many inequalities would simply disappear. Therefore, when we discuss race, we may feel like we are perpetuating inequalities by talking about it at all. However, this ignores two key points: race isn't the only axis on which inequality occurs, and racial differences can be positive too.

As we discussed in the previous chapter, privilege and inequalities are not an exclusively race-based issue. The world is not so simplistic. There are disparities in the experiences of people of different genders, sexual orientations, physical and cognitive abilities, religions, and socio-economic statuses. To single out race and decide it is the only thing that's not allowed to be talked about is to ignore these other opportunities for prejudice to occur and to unfairly demonize race.

Race is also valuable to discuss, not just for the negative ways in which it can affect people's lives, but the positive ways too. Many people feel like their racial communities are an intrinsic part of who they are. They wouldn't wish to be any other race in the world, regardless of privileges, because they like their traditions and sense of community. This is the idea motivating things like the "Black Is Beautiful" campaign, which promotes self-love and respect, and heritage months that focus on the histories and lived experiences of different racial and cultural groups. There is a great deal to be proud of in the creations of every race, from food, to music, to scientific inventions, to art, and much more. There's also a lot to learn about historical figures from groups who are too often excluded from textbooks and classrooms. If you want your diversity and inclusion strategy to really shine, invite conversations about race that discuss its positive aspects as often as you talk about its negative impacts. Race isn't a bad thing, and treating it like some taboo that no one is allowed to speak of does a lot to harm the idea that people of every race have something to bring to the table.

Some people will point to the discomfort that discussions about race cause and say this is enough of a reason to leave these kinds of conversations out of professional settings. However, consider whose comfort is really being protected here. Are the people who are being negatively impacted by prejudiced ways of thinking more comfortable with not talking about how racism can harm them? Are they better off completely ignoring their background and culture, even if it may be a benefit to their team? In most cases, when we seek to avoid causing discomfort, we only do so for the people who are privileged enough to ignore how race affects their lives. This isn't true comfort, and it contributes to holding up the current power structure without fixing any of the inequalities inherent in it. It is necessary for those in power to feel discomfort so that they can recognize what is wrong and bring about change. If they can remain comfortable and never address any of the realities of race, everything will remain exactly as it is, as there won't be any pressure to fix it. The power of discomfort is discussed in more detail in Chapter 12.

We'll start by taking a look at some of the primary reasons why discussions of race can cause discomfort. These include revealing truths that we otherwise might be ignorant of, holding tough conversations about how some people benefit from systemic racism and the power it confers, and the tendency for some to get defensive when talking explicitly about the effects of race within a society.

Shining a Spotlight on Unspoken Truths

It is much easier to ignore a problem when it goes unspoken. Without talking about things like prejudice and discrimination, they can go on unaddressed for months or years. It can be difficult to talk about the ways that racial discrimination affects people's lives, and many would prefer to never or only rarely mention it. These are topics that are difficult to address, and you might be worried you'll bring an issue to light that is tough to accept.

While acknowledging these issues is hard, failing to acknowledge them doesn't make them go away. Just because you ignore an issue doesn't mean it ceases to exist. This can often make it worse, as you have the ability to help and you choose not to just to avoid a difficult conversation. The truth may be a hard pill to swallow sometimes, especially if it means admitting you might have been complacent in allowing injustice to continue within your group, purposefully or not. But if you do not confront the truth, you won't be able to do anything to further your inclusivity efforts and correct any issues that may be present within the organization.

Failing to talk about the harsh realities of racism, including the ways racial bias can seep into policies and behaviors without your explicit notice, gives them a free pass to continue. When you start having conversations as a group about how race affects interactions between team members and who is able to be successful within your team, you can turn unspoken truths into acknowledged ones, which means you can start working on a plan to fix them. Good communication is absolutely imperative to solving problems on both individual and systemic levels.

Revealing a Lack of Knowledge

It can be difficult to admit when you are wrong or ignorant about a topic. As a leader, you may worry that showcasing how little you know about a given topic might undermine people's faith in you as well. For example, no one wants to find out that the CEO of their company has no idea how payroll works, since even if you don't take care of it yourself, you should have a good idea of the process for better management. But how does this fear of a lack of knowledge apply in regards to discussions of race?

Discussions about race can bring up topics such as privileges that you don't have personal experience with or cultural touchstones that are only familiar to people within that group. You might not feel fully equipped to navigate them if you're not experienced in having these kinds of conversations. You might worry you'll say the wrong thing and come off as insensitive, or that others won't trust you to be a good leader if you admit you don't know everything. This is an especially relevant concern if you are part of the racial majority group, as you don't have firsthand experience of what it's like to be a minority. Because of this, you may simply choose not to talk about race at all, so as not to reveal the gaps in your knowledge.

This kind of thinking is counterproductive, as it prevents you from ever learning what you don't know. If you never talk about race, you won't ever learn about the experiences of people from different racial groups. You'll always be in the dark, which is much more harmful than coming off as ignorant for a few minutes before being informed of whatever information you were missing. If you are worried about knowing too little to talk about race confidently, that is all the more reason to hear others' opinions and perspectives. Remember that facilitating the conversation doesn't mean you have to lead it. Take an active listening role if you don't feel like you have the authority to speak on an issue, and be open to learning new information, even if it means you have to find out just how little you know in the process.

Defensive Reactions

Just like many of the other conversations about diversity we have discussed so far, discussions about race are often held up by defensive reactions. This is an extension of the idea that by pointing out differences in how people of each race experience the world, blame is being laid at the feet of the people who benefit from the system. It's possible that white people having serious conversations about racial bias for the first time may feel like they are being treated with hostility or told that it's their fault that systemic inequalities exist. While everyone is responsible for doing their part to be inclusive and antiracist, systemic biases cannot be attributed to a single person, so no one should be made to feel like they are the root cause of discrimination. However, refusing to take part in conversations about race or getting overly defensive could create a roadblock that prevents change from occurring. Therefore, it is important that no one is made to feel like they're to blame for more systemic issues.

To avoid these reactions and make sure everyone is on the same page when it comes to eliminating racial bias, you'll sometimes need to walk a tightrope between outright accusing people of bigotry and being too lenient, letting unacceptable behaviors slide. These are uncomfortable conversations to have, but with the right skills, you should be able to navigate them without issue.

Holding Uncomfortable Conversations

We tend to gravitate toward resisting discomfort wherever we can in our lives. We might let something that frustrates us continue just for the sake of avoiding an argument. When we choose to ignore these issues rather than address them, the behavior that bothers us typically only gets worse. More often than not, our resentment grows, until one day we can't take it anymore and explode. Now, instead of having a terse but fairly calm discussion about why something bothered us and what could be done to fix the situation, we end up unable to control our outburst. We end up in a more distressing situation, all because we wanted to avoid discomfort so badly.

The real value of uncomfortable conversations is that they allow us to skip this messy outcome by catching problems early, before they can fester. One awkward confrontation is far less painful than months or years of lingering discrimination that goes unaddressed. While these conversations are important, that doesn't mean they're easy. Missteps may only serve to further alienate some people who weren't completely on board in the first place, and some may resist or object to proposed changes that either don't benefit them or take away some of the privileges they have previously enjoyed. If you're going to have these conversations, you might face some pushback, which you need to know how to handle. The art of managing uncomfortable conversations is a tricky one to be sure, but it's entirely possible for everyone to learn.

When discussing race in the workplace or another group setting, pay attention to two primary considerations. The first is making an effort to involve everyone in these discussions, avoiding the problems inherent with singling out only white people or only people of color. The second is handling objections in a way that lets the objector's concerns feel validated while still assuring them that this is the best possible solution for everyone.

Including Everyone When Discussing Race

Too often, discussions about race seem to happen within racial groups rather than between them. People experiencing racial bias might discuss it with other people of color who have personally experienced what they've gone through, or they might be tasked with leading diversity committees with almost no involvement from white people. White people might talk about the need for diversity and possible ways to create a more inclusive environment, but fail to get input from people of color, so these policies fall short of their goals. The most effective way to see significant change in how your organization handles issues surrounding race is to get everyone involved in the same conversation. Create task forces that are just as racially diverse as the company. Involve people of color in your meetings and discussions so they can share their perspectives. When everyone collaborates, you'll have the greatest diversity of thought, and you'll demonstrate that inclusivity applies to everyone. White people can and should be involved in discussions about race so they can feel fully supportive of any inclusivity policies that are proposed, and people of color can and should tell their stories and speak from their perspectives to guide the conversation.

Dealing with Objections

Objections to conversations about race can come from both the people experiencing racially-motivated prejudice and those who may be unconsciously participating in it. Some people who have enjoyed the privilege of not ever being judged based on their race may have a limited perspective that keeps them from seeing the value of these conversations. They may argue that they're not purposefully being racist, and therefore they shouldn't need to change anything about their behaviors. They may also say the topic makes them uncomfortable, or that subtler forms of inequality like microaggressions and unconscious bias aren't that big a deal. On the other hand, people who have experienced discrimination may be equally reluctant to talk about race, as they feel like the pain they have experienced isn't appropriate for discussion or debate. Alternatively, they may have internalized biases that complicate their ability to recognize the way racism affects them.

Dealing with these objections requires you to be sensitive and considerate of others' feelings when they resist these uncomfortable topics. Try to understand why they might shy away from talking about race, and do your best to explain why it's a necessary conversation to have while assuaging their fears. Help them see that they may still be complicit in systems that uphold racism, even if they are not trying to be racist themselves, and explain the harm that ignoring and overlooking these tough topics causes. Treat testimonials with the respect they deserve, and try not to turn anyone's lived experiences into a topic of debate. Work to gradually introduce concepts like internalized bias and systemic oppression to those who might not have encountered them before so that when they come up in conversations, they will not feel like accusations. Above all else, treat everyone on your team like a human being and try to meet them on their level. The more respectful you are to them, being understanding and accommodating of their concerns while remaining firm in your own arguments, the better they'll be able to participate in talks about race without worry, fear, or frustration.

Chapter 12: Real Discomfort Transcends into Real Change

If people with the power to affect policies and company culture are given the opportunity to remain complacent about diversity issues, there's a good chance nothing will change. However, when pressure is applied and discomfort is introduced into the equation, this is when real, lasting change becomes possible. To understand this, you need look no further than the widespread protest movement in 2020 that involved not just people in the U.S. fighting against systemic forms of oppression that affect black people, but also in Canada and many other parts of the world. These protests were far from comfortable, with many involving hundreds or even thousands of people. They could not be ignored, and yet that was exactly what made them so effective in capturing the public's attention and drawing a great deal of support.

Protests have long been a tool used by those experiencing oppression specifically because they invite discussion through disruption. If no one knows there is a significant-enough problem that people are willing to come out in droves and join together to draw attention to it, then the issues in question will be overlooked again and again, and the problems will continue. Through protest and other forms of activism, discomfort spawns real conversations about racism, bigotry, and diversity that might have otherwise gone unsaid.

Of course, protests aren't the only way to disrupt complacency. Other methods like awareness campaigns and petitioning governments also work to bring the issue into the public eye. Sometimes, having a conversation with someone who has lived a vastly different life from yours is enough to create the discomfort necessary to open your eyes to the reality of others' experiences. It is only by speaking with and listening to people who have experienced oppression firsthand that you can truly claim to understand their point of view. Having authentic discussions with people different from yourself can serve as the spark that lights the flame of change, all because you didn't shy away from heavy topics and hard questions.

The Necessity of Hard Questions

Consider this scenario: you're a student in a class and you have a test coming up. You find out that the questions on the test are all going to be very easy, and you could answer most of them without having to think too long on your response or look for a more out-of-the-box solution. How hard do you think you would study for that class? How much effort would you put into getting a good grade? If you're not being tested and challenged on your knowledge, then why bother to learn more than the bare minimum anyway?

If you don't ask the hard questions in life, you probably won't ever seriously consider issues of inclusivity and prejudice either. If you have no reason to become a more socially conscious individual, then why would you? Many people simply don't. They never have to face discrimination, or they convince themselves that the discrimination they face isn't so bad, and so they don't dwell on it. They don't have answers for hard questions because they've never really been asked to think about them. In other words, they don't have to study for their "class," because no one's asking them questions anyway.

When we ask hard questions like what it means to be diverse, how we can be more inclusive, and what we can do to be better allies to those in need of our support, we test ourselves. We motivate ourselves to study, through our own research or through talking about these issues with others. We start to care about how well we can answer these kinds of questions. It is our discomfort at not knowing the answers that drives us to pursue knowledge in all its forms. When we are uncomfortable, we learn, grow, and adapt to our ever-changing world much more readily than we would if there was no pressure on us to improve. Comfort is the antithesis to change, because if we were comfortable, we would never change.

There is very little need to change things if we are comfortable with them. You probably wouldn't rush out to the store to buy a new mattress if your current one wasn't full of lumps and bumps from overuse.

The money and effort that you'd put into buying the mattress just wouldn't be worth it. This applies to other areas of life as well, including efforts to improve diversity and inclusion. If a policy that is based in prejudice doesn't directly affect you, and no one ever brings up the harm it's causing to others, you might not even realize it needs to be changed. Even if you did recognize its faults, you might still decide that it would be too troublesome to rework the old policy and decide to just keep it around.

This all changes when you have honest, often uncomfortable conversations about how these policies affect others. When you recognize the damage they can do, it's no longer comfortable to keep them around or to pretend like they don't do any harm. You recognize that by failing to make a group as inclusive as possible, you are making it an uncomfortable place for many people to be. This then motivates you to put in the effort and time required to change the policy, where your previous comfortable perspective did not.

The connection between comfort and compliance is exactly why awareness campaigns can be so powerful. When you don't know about the difficult realities of many people's situations, you might not feel motivated to do anything to fix them. When others make you aware of these difficulties, you become committed to assisting in the effort to rectify them. When you discuss issues like racism, sexism, homophobia, and ableism with your team, don't shy away from the topics that provoke the most discomfort. Be honest without sugarcoating the reality of the situation. This discomfort is incredibly valuable.

The Value of Discomfort

If comfort is responsible for compliance, then discomfort is responsible for efforts to improve the situation for everyone. When you're uncomfortable, you want to return to those feelings of comfort you previously enjoyed. If the recognition of prejudice has made you uncomfortable, this is a good thing. It means you are no longer content to allow this to continue, and you are ready to make the changes necessary to help everyone have a comfortable experience at work, within the classroom, or in another group setting.

The value of discomfort is closely related to the concept of delayed gratification. Typically, we tend to gravitate toward things that offer us instant gratification. We might make purchases to improve our mood, or consume sugar, caffeine, and junk food. These are short-term solutions that are relatively painless and keep us comfortable, but they don't actually solve the problem in the long term. Delayed gratification involves accepting that you are uncomfortable now but that it is okay to remain uncomfortable for a while if you can get a better outcome later on. For example, you might look at the reasons underlying your unhappiness and try to address them rather than slapping the equivalent of a bandage on a bullet wound. You might try to really experience these unpleasant feelings and understand where they're coming from so you can target the source of the problem, enjoying more long-lasting positivity as a result. You'll need to accept that you may be uncomfortable for a while, but it's in the service of finding a more profound, permanent feeling of comfort.

Diversity and inclusion efforts can benefit from the delayed gratification principle as well. Pretending inequalities do not exist or trying to fix them with policies that amount to little more than lip service and good publicity brings you back into comfort faster, serving as a type of instant gratification. But these kinds of efforts don't really address the root of the problem. Instead, by embracing the discomfort required to fully understand the extent to which these policies can be harmful, you can put in the effort to really fix them. Eventually, you will achieve a more permanent solution that makes everyone comfortable, all because you refused to shy away from the uncomfortable truths.

Recognizing the Flaws in the System

It's often hard to accept that a system you have been contributing to has been hurting others. If someone points out how a policy is discriminatory, you might not want to listen at first. You may not even give them the chance to speak because you are worried about what they're going to say. If you ignore these issues and continue to insist that everything is fine, you might avoid some discomfort on your end, but what about the discomfort that others experience every day from these harmful attitudes?

To turn a blind eye to the flaws in the system is to play an active role in perpetuating them. If you refuse to listen to others when they say a practice or an aspect of company culture is hurting them, you effectively participate in hurting them. It's a refusal to help when you know there is something you could do to ease their suffering, and it can stem, consciously or unconsciously, from the desire to avoid conflict and discomfort.

There are many ways to become more familiar with any flaws that may exist in your leadership strategy or management style in regards to diversity and inclusion. The first is to be open always to criticism and advice from those who are experiencing issues. Make it convenient for people to talk directly to you about the problems they are facing, and show them you care about their input. You could set aside a portion of your day as "office hours," where you put down your regular work and give your team members your full attention. You can be more present in the office or at the group meetings if you typically work from home or only spend a few hours around the rest of your team. If you have an office, you might even consider moving it to be closer to other employees. This makes you seem more approachable and accessible, removing some of the barriers that might keep people from reporting bad interactions they've had.

Being open and accessible is just one thing you can do to encourage feedback. In some circumstances, you may need to actively seek it out instead of just waiting for it. This is necessary if people still feel uncomfortable about discussing these issues. Hold monthly meetings where you talk opening about inclusivity and what you can do to support it. Offer people an anonymous way to report issues to you, such as a complaint box or an online form that doesn't ask for their name. Anonymity can help reduce fears that they will experience retaliation for pointing out a problem or talking about a specific person or incident that has made them uncomfortable. It is a great way to warm everyone up to the idea of talking about the injustices they have experienced without putting them on the spot or turning them into a target for backlash.

Each of these methods of gathering feedback is a great way to help you see where some of the biggest flaws lie in the systems you currently use. Without feedback, and without the willingness to engage in uncomfortable conversations, these systems can continue without meaningful critique. As you seek out more feedback from the people on your team and get comfortable with the idea of discomfort, you will be more motivated than ever to make significant changes that have a strong positive effect on everyone's experiences.

Spurring Change

Despite the best of intentions, real change is sometimes very hard to accept. We are often creatures of habit, and we tend to avoid anything that makes us change too much about our daily routines and the procedures we are used to following. Sometimes, this can be a good thing. It helps us derive comfort from our daily routines and keeps us from getting too stressed in an ever-changing environment. However, in the case of diversity and inclusion efforts, it can also be rather troublesome, as we need to work against our nature to fix issues that could otherwise linger for months or years. In order to implement inclusivity policies, we have to be comfortable with the discomfort that change produces.

There are a few ways you can warm yourself and your team members up to the idea of change. The first is by being clear and explaining all the ways things will be different. A fear of change can often come from the fear of the unknown. You don't know what things will be like if you change the system, but you do know what they're like right now. Because of this, you might be tempted to stick with "the devil you know" rather than venturing off into the unknown. But if you always stuck with what you knew, you would never make improvements. When people know exactly what a given change entails and how it will affect them, they can feel better prepared for the change. Nothing will feel like it's being suddenly sprung on them. Instead, they can gradually adjust to what's new and accept the changes in their routines, which makes them more palatable.

Another important measure is showcasing the benefits of change. It's easy to fixate on the potential drawbacks, and these tend to stick out first as people look for reasons to avoid and push back against change. If you want everything to stay the same, you'll immediately jump to listing all the ways in which any change could go horribly wrong. But in the case of diversity and inclusion efforts, the potential cons pale in comparison to the many pros. These include the benefits discussed in Chapter 4 such as better problem-solving and creativity, more engagement at work, and a more community feel within an organization. These are huge benefits and they apply to everyone, not just those who were previously disadvantaged by non-inclusive policies. Emphasize the benefits, and people will quickly see how they eclipse the few possible downsides.

Praise is a powerful tool in your arsenal as well. Criticism can make people reflexively frustrated with change. If they feel like they are being forced to change, or if they are told that what they are currently doing is wrong and shamed for it, they're probably not going to listen to all the reasons that the change is for the better. They may even go out of their way to be outspokenly against change because they feel defensive and hurt by these allegations. Instead of relying on critique, embrace praise as a more powerful motivator. When you see people sticking to the new inclusivity policies or practicing inclusion on their own, commend them for it with a kind word or gesture. Let people feel like they're having a positive effect on the group through their willingness to change, and use positive reinforcement to show them they're on the right path. When people feel good about the work they're doing, they're more likely to stick to it.

You can also ease the transition by facilitating forgiveness. We all make mistakes. From time to time, we all say or do things we didn't mean to be harmful, and yet they cause harm. If someone was previously holding up old policies that got in the way of inclusivity but has since changed their tune, there's no point in shaming them for their past actions. Of course, they must be genuine in their remorse and fully committed to making a positive change, but once they show they want to improve and be part of the new inclusivity efforts, it helps no one to continue to exclude or shame them. Practice forgiveness for errors that were made out of ignorance rather than malice, and educate rather than continuing to lay blame. Once a problem has been corrected and the change has been made, there is no more need for hard feelings.

Finally, when committing to change, don't forget to set goals. Look to the future and envision the type of inclusive community you'd like your company or group to be. Think about the kind of interactions you want to see and the level of diversity you want to achieve. Set specific goals, like having at least 40% of your workforce be diverse in some way, or committing to considering at least one female employee for a promotion if everyone else at that level of upper management is male. You can also set goals for employee attitudes on feedback reports, such as getting at least 80% to respond that they think the company is very inclusive. Once you reach these goals, celebrate them with your whole team, so everyone gets to feel like they had a hand in accomplishing something great.

Chapter 13: What Does Inclusionary Change Look Like in Leadership?

We've talked at length about the importance of being inclusive and making changes in the service of greater inclusivity, but what exactly should those changes be? In this chapter, we're going to focus on specific changes and goals you can use as you make improvements to inclusivity. As the leader of your group, organization, or company, you take on the burden of the responsibility for shepherding in inclusionary change. By working to make your team more diverse and intervening to prevent actions and mindsets motivated by prejudice from taking hold, you lead the way in important inclusivity efforts.

Inclusive leadership takes many forms. It involves expanding diversity and inclusivity efforts to include administrative roles, management positions, and other positions of power. It is not enough to simply have people of color in the company; they must be included at all levels of management so you get just as many diverse perspectives for every aspect of the organization. Inclusive leadership also works to shine a spotlight on inclusivity, always actively looking for ways to improve everyone's experiences and never resting on your laurels or deciding that you've done "good enough" when there are still lingering issues. Being an inclusive leader means acknowledging resistance to change while committing yourself to it, carving a path that others can follow. It means setting a good example, taking an active listening role and showing others what it means to be a good ally. You'll need to create spaces that empower team members, helping them feel safe and trusting to facilitate potentially uncomfortable conversations. You're also responsible for guiding company culture through both your words and actions.

Without a doubt, inclusive leadership demands hard work and commitment. It requires you to step up to the plate and go above and beyond the bare minimum requirements laid out by diversity laws. It's not enough to just comply with standards set by others and decide you've done enough, not when it means that some people may still be struggling with feelings of exclusion and distress. Great leaders are willing to take every necessary step to ensure everyone feels included and no one is made to feel ashamed or inconvenienced by who they are. As you begin implementing the tenets of inclusive leadership into your life and daily practices, you'll see firsthand just how completely revolutionary they can be.

Diversity in Leadership Roles

One of the key things to consider when increasing the amount of diversity in your company is how that diversity is reflected in your leadership roles. You might have a lot of diversity at the ground level, but company culture may be more monolithic as you travel up the corporate ladder. This is a key concern for two reasons. The first is that this shows a commitment to inclusion that goes far beyond lip service or empty gestures. If you are willing to make people with diverse backgrounds and ways of thinking about issues your top-level managers and closest advisers, this tells others you are willing to listen to people with points of view other than your own and seriously consider their opinions on issues. The second is that the people in upper management roles generally have more influence on company policies, and having more diversity here means non-inclusive policies and prejudices are caught and dealt with faster.

Having a highly diverse company is great, but if that diversity is only present for entry-level positions and significantly lacking from the more influential roles, it may come across more as trying to fill a quota than actually trying to yield positive change. Many of the people who are furthest down the company ladder are new hires who haven't been with the company long, or who may not remain in their positions for multiple years. Even in other organizations, these people often end up doing the bulk of the grunt work, typically being told what to do with the expectation that they will follow these instructions with few questions. If you're really working to be more inclusive, it might not be a good idea to confine all of your diversity to these lower-level positions, as they don't have any real control over how the company is run and they are the most likely to be hit hard by non-inclusive policies. Additionally, if people see that non-white employees aren't included in management positions, they will probably assume that they're not likely to get a promotion anytime soon. They may feel as though there's no point in trying to have their ideas heard, as they lack the standing in the company for their voice to make a difference. These attitudes may persist whether or not you use methods like feedback surveys to gauge the effectiveness of inclusivity policies. If you're not careful, you could end up with a revolving door where diverse hires leave as quickly as they come when they realize there is little to no upward momentum for them at the company. This means you're not building a consistent, reliable team interested in working together in the long-term and coming together as one community, and it can leave people of different races, religions, and sexual orientations feeling isolated from their peers.

When you fill your upper management with as much diversity as every other area of your company, you have a much better chance of possible barriers to inclusion being brought to your attention. Someone working as a salesperson might not have the tools or the influence to change company policy or affect the attitudes of other employees, but someone working in an administrative or HR role absolutely can. Their jobs give them a way to routinely report back to you about any issues other team members are experiencing and to hold you accountable for addressing these issues in an equitable way. Diversity at all levels is absolutely mandatory for an inclusive company.

Even though diversity is growing within many companies, it's important to pay attention to where this diversity is occurring. The disparity between diversity and inclusion in lower-level and upper-level positions is readily apparent. For example, a survey of U.S. hospitality companies found that while "54% of our respondents say the industry presents equal opportunities regardless of an employee's race, religion, national origin, gender, ability, or age," there is still a significant disparity in upper-level management, with "80.9% of hospitality management positions held by White workers, versus the 7% held by Black or African American workers." Additionally, The U.S. Equal Opportunity Commission actually found that diversity in upper management positions has been on the decline, as "in 2007, 29% of upper management positions were held by people of color and in 2015, it decreased to 19%" (Hcareers, 2020, para. 4-5). This is a significant difference and a troubling trend. Even as companies have greater diversity, this diversity isn't reflected in its leadership, which means the changes in hiring standards and policies are not truly equitable across the board.

Be especially cognizant of these issues within your own leadership. Pay attention to the proportion of people at each level of the company who are not from majority demographics, and see what you can do to correct these issues while still finding the right people for the job. Consider promoting people from within the company rather than hiring from outside the company to fill leadership roles, but if you feel that you're lacking in diversity, don't be afraid to expand your hiring criteria when necessary. Rest assured that there are perfectly capable candidates for all positions who are a part of different racial, ethnic, and religious groups, and that recruiting diversely in upper-level positions will only ever benefit your team.

On the other hand, tokenism is a form of diversity that largely focuses on keeping up appearances of being diverse while failing to actually be inclusive. It involves a more symbolic, outward-facing attempt to be diverse that does very little to help the organization experience the real benefits of diverse voices. A company that practices tokenism might hire a small handful of people of color in minor roles throughout their organization, then brush off their hands and declare that they're very committed to diversity efforts. It's a way to do the bare minimum without really having to put any effort into inclusivity, and it doesn't yield much positive change.

How many times have you watched a show that has a nearly all-white cast with just a single black person? What about an all-male cast with one or two women in supporting roles? Maybe you've seen shows where the main character has a "gay best friend" who seems to only be there to provide support, and who never gets a love interest of their own. These shows all perpetuate tokenism. They give the audience a "token" character from a demographic other than straight, white, and male, largely so they can claim their show is diverse without really putting in any effort to flesh these characters out the same way they do with their leading roles. Worse, you've probably seen examples of some common media tropes that make the portrayal of these token characters even more egregious. These include the tendency for shows to kill off their only gay characters or to cast people of color in support roles where their plotlines only revolve around what other people are doing. By reducing minority characters to less significant parts and failing to draw any focus to them, showrunners are attempting to garner praise for being diverse without understanding why diversity is so important and beneficial in the first place.

These shows and characters are not real, of course, but they reflect the very real way that the people who write and direct them think about race and diversity and how our society as a whole view these issues. Tokenism inherently perpetuates stereotypes, as it suggests that a single person from any demographic is enough to represent an entire race, religion, culture, or identity. It implies that everyone from that group acts and thinks the same way, and when it's the only representation available, it can affect the way people from outside that group think of people different from themselves. It also showcases the ways some people believe diversity just means checking a certain number of boxes, then sidelining these people rather than actually listening to their different perspectives. Tokenism can be almost as harmful as having no diversity at all, as just because people of different cultures are present, that doesn't mean they're being listened to or valued. This lack of inclusivity can completely defeat the point of having a more diverse team.

If you want to avoid the trap of tokenism, consider how you approach diversity. Are you treating it like a checklist you have to do, or are you actually invested in the various perspectives that greater diversity brings to the table? Are you trying to show off your handful of employees of color and use them to deflect criticisms of a lack of inclusion, or are they team members like anyone else? Do you stage publicity photos in a way that showcases diversity, or are your teams naturally diverse enough that you don't need to? Do you rely on a single person to serve as a representative for the thoughts and opinions of their race, or are you inviting in different perspectives from people within the same demographic group? Do you only think of your own needs when providing accommodations for your team members, or do you go out of your way to include appropriate measures for people with different dietary, religious, and lifestyle needs? Evaluate your diversity measures by these standards, identifying where you have already made great strides and where you need to improve. This will keep you from hiring to fill quotas or using paltry efforts at diversity as a shield to deflect criticisms, thus avoiding tokenism.

Lifting Up Minority Voices

Including people in minority groups in your company or group is one thing, but actually giving them a space where they feel comfortable to voice their opinions is another. Additionally, you'll need to ensure that these perspectives are given enough weight that they can actually affect policies and decision-making. It doesn't matter if someone is an expert in their field if you never take their advice into account. It won't be of any help to you if you don't listen to it, and in order to do this, you'll need to make an effort to lift up minority voices.

Too often, people in minority groups are talked over or discouraged from contributing. They aren't asked for their opinion, and when they are, their perspectives are often treated as lesser or more limited compared to the opinions of people from cultural majority groups. If this is allowed to continue, it can completely defeat the purpose of diversity. There is no point in recruiting people from different walks of life if you don't give them a platform from which to speak and the resources to act on their ideas. Make sure that everyone on your team feels like their opinions are valued and that they're not just allowed but encouraged to join the conversation. Without giving people in minority groups a voice within your team, you cannot truly say you're inclusive.

Being a Leader for Inclusionary Change

Diversity is only one part of the equation. Inclusive practices are also necessary when leading the way to positive change in your organization. Inclusivity efforts are where the changes you make to your policies and attitudes really shine, as well as where most people on the team take their cues for appropriate and inclusive behavior. By dedicating yourself to encouraging change, creating safe environments, listening to those who have personally experienced discrimination, being a good ally, and guiding the development of organizational culture, you utilize an effective inclusivity strategy that creates powerful, long-lasting changes.

Acknowledging Any Deep-Seated Resistance to Change

Change rarely occurs without barriers and resistance. If you are trying to alter attitudes and behaviors that people have held for years, sometimes even their entire lives, this is, understandably, not always going to be an easy task. In previous chapters, you've learned about some of the possible causes of resistance, such as limited perspectives and privilege, fear, leaping to assumptions, and defensiveness. You've also learned how to respond to many of them, by presenting the benefits of the new changes, listening to people's concerns, reassuring them that these changes won't lead to the manifestation of their worst fears, and involving even your greatest dissenters in your efforts to be more inclusive. It's not always easy to overturn people's resistance to change, but it is a necessary step if you want your inclusivity strategy to really take root throughout the entire group.

A chain is only as strong as its weakest link, as the old saying goes. If negative attitudes toward change are allowed to persist, they can slowly pervade the whole company, eliminating the excitement many team members might have had and quickly turning it to fear and mistrust. You can't force everyone to be happy with the idea of change, but you can do everything in your power to ease the transition. This starts with education and maintaining your own positive attitude, as well as talking to the team members who are the greatest sources of discontent. Acknowledge their concerns, and kindly but firmly explain why inclusivity is necessary and beneficial. Turning a blind eye to resistance to change does nothing to help people feel more comfortable with it. It is only by addressing this discomfort that you can start to alleviate it and pave the way to real change.

Making a Commitment to Being an Instrument of Change

Attitudes toward change within your team are largely contingent on your own attitude. If you treat diversity and inclusion like unfortunate tasks you have to complete and pay them as little attention as possible, other team members will start to see them this way as well. They won't be invested in supporting these efforts, and while changes might be made, they likely won't be full changes necessary to make anyone really feel included. If people from minority groups in your company or group feel like they're only there to fill a quota, their discomfort might cause them to leave and find somewhere else where they feel more accepted. On the other hand, if you are enthusiastic about change and you try to encourage it everywhere you can, people will pick up on this positivity instead. They might temper their initial doubts because you've made the idea of change sound like such a great thing. They may even find that your dedication is infectious and feel more strongly about diversity and inclusion efforts themselves. This is a much better attitude for everyone to have, and it all stems from your own attitude.

Change is most effective when everyone is on board and has an emotional investment in the results. By drumming up excitement about new changes, whether through announcing them in an energetic and optimistic way or by effectively explaining all the benefits people can enjoy thanks to these changes, focusing on the pros rather than the drawbacks, you can inspire confidence in not just these changes but also your abilities as a leader.

Creating Safe Spaces and a Supportive Environment

The phrase "safe space" has become a topic of controversy in some circles, but this is largely the result of a misunderstanding about its meaning. Creating a safe space doesn't mean that there are no conflicts, no serious issues can be discussed, or that difficult topics are completely excluded. In fact, it's quite the opposite. A safe space is simply a place where every member of the group feels comfortable to be themselves without fear of judgment. When you create real spaces of safety and inclusion, you can facilitate conversations about even the most difficult and uncomfortable topics, like racism, prejudice, and discrimination.

The office or meeting space for your group should serve as a safe space for your team. If someone feels uncomfortable to express themselves, they'll be distracted by these feelings, and they won't be able to put their full focus into their work. They may feel disconnected from their teammates, and they're more likely to shy away from providing their input and perspective. This can interfere with collaborating and problem-solving, as their voices are suppressed. However, when everyone feels safe enough that they don't fear being outcast or judged for their differences, they can be more honest and open when discussing these differences. They can bring their unique perspective to the table, and they can talk with authority on topics in which they have firsthand experience thanks to their social or cultural background. By creating a safe space that is inclusive for all, you give everyone a location where they are unafraid to have authentic and brave conversations about their experiences and points of view.

Practicing Active Listening

Many companies hire diverse employees, but they only listen to their suggestions and perspectives passively. This is listening without the intention to react to or act on what you are hearing. For example, if someone starts chattering away about a topic you're not very interested in, you might tune them out, offering half-hearted responses and not internalizing anything you're being told. This is fine for casual conversation, but it should have no place within a productive team. Passive listening implies you don't really care about what someone is saying, and it's not going to affect your actions. If you only listen passively to people who have different viewpoints from your own, nothing will change, since you won't actually be learning anything.

Active listening, on the other hand, is listening with the intention to learn and grow. It involves giving someone your full focus when they're talking, and also contributing to the conversation yourself. Additionally, active listening means paying attention to nonverbal cues as well so you can understand someone's complete message. For example, someone might say a certain policy doesn't bother or target them, but their body language might indicate otherwise. If you're only passively listening, you might not pick up on this. With active listening, you pay more attention to verbal and nonverbal cues, giving you a better understanding of what someone is saying.

In regards to diversity and inclusion, active listening also means listening with the intention to take action once someone brings up an issue. If a team member feels like a policy is discriminatory, you must take action and address it. Without this key step, people won't really feel like they've been heard, since nothing will change. This doesn't mean you have to unquestioningly act on every suggestion one of your team members makes. You can still use your judgment to decide where and when to intervene. Still, being an active listener requires you to be ready to act when it's appropriate and obligates you to challenge any biases that might make you resistant to hearing someone else's perspective on an issue. Give important conversations your attention, take the time to really hear and understand what someone is saying, and propose a solution rather than brushing concerns aside.

Defining the Role of an Ally

If you are not a member of a certain minority group, you can still lend them your support and advocate alongside them. This is known as being an ally. Since you have more control in your organization than any other team members, it is very important for you to act in support of oppressed groups, whether or not you are a part of them. Being a good ally means listening to the voices of people who have experienced discrimination, lifting up their stories of these experiences and their recommendations for eliminating these issues, and furthering their cause to be treated fairly and equitably.

Be careful to avoid expressions of performative allyship. These are words and actions that check all the right boxes in terms of sounding progressive and supportive, but actually do little to advance a given cause. For example, some companies will produce limited-time rainbow packages for their products for pride month, but they will be silent about issues the LGBT community faces during all other months of the year. They may also have company policies that unfairly target their own LGBT employees, like not giving same-sex partners the same benefits as married couples or restricting the display of pride flags within the office. These companies have the outward appearance of being supportive, but none of the internal changes that would really matter. They want to be part of the celebration, and they are fine marketing to LGBT consumers by coming across as their allies, but their actual words and actions never really lead to any sort of positive change or greater acceptance. They get the benefits of appearing to be inclusive without doing any of the hard work involved in actually being inclusive.

It's fine to engage in public displays of support and to celebrate diversity, but this shouldn't be where your allyship ends. Set a positive example for other potential allies within the company by showing them how to lend their support. Encourage people to engage in hands-on work. Facilitate difficult conversations and serve as an educational resource for people who might not fully understand the complexities of issues like racism and sexism, while deferring to those who have experienced it when you aren't entirely certain of something. Do the right thing, even when it's not the popular thing to do, simply because it's right. These are all ways to be a good ally. The more you practice them, the more everyone on your team will learn to be good allies for each other too.

Changing Company Culture

As mentioned previously, company culture will develop whether you're there to guide it or not. If you let negative attitudes about diversity and inclusion to persist without being challenged, it won't be surprising when these ideas spread throughout the entire group. This can lead to increased tensions between team members and greater resistance to inclusivity strategies when you try to implement them.

In order to redirect team culture and make attitudes more supportive and inclusive, you'll need to lead the way. A positive attitude can be infectious, and your full commitment to being more inclusive will help others understand that this is something that matters to you personally, making it matter to them too. Good communication is imperative, as is providing motivators to engage in the company culture. Use different incentives that appeal to different people. Extrinsic motivators that involve tangible rewards like bonuses or consideration for a management role when team members demonstrate they're committed to inclusivity too are fine, but don't forget about intrinsic motivators that appeal to people's senses of pride and accomplishment. These include gestures like recognizing team members who go out of their way to be inclusive and finding ways to make inclusivity fun through company bonding games and exercises. The more your company culture grows to reflect inclusivity, the easier it will be to change outdated policies and embrace inclusivity everywhere from management to new hires.

Chapter 14: Developing Inclusive Leadership Practices

At this point, you understand the basics of the importance of diversity and inclusion on their own merits, as well as the ways they can work for your company. You've also learned about what it takes to be an inclusive leader who supports their team in terms of your attitude and how you approach these issues. All that is left is for you is to focus on creating and implementing leadership practices that facilitate diversity.

In some respects, this can feel a little like striking out on your own. As mentioned in Chapter 6, diversity and inclusion aren't typically considered core leadership competencies, though this may change over the years as the need for these strategies becomes more apparent. You may feel like you don't have enough experience or worry about having ineffective methods because you haven't been formally trained in implementing inclusive policies. Even though you might feel out of your element, you shouldn't shy away from such an important step in making your group more inclusive. Having the right attitude is great, but attitude is meaningless if effective policies aren't there to back it up.

Your policies have a significant impact on eliminating biases on both the systemic and individual levels.

Policies and practices that uphold prejudices, rely on stereotypes, and mishandle diversity and inclusion methods don't help anyone feel more like they're part of a team. Instead, they only serve to isolate team members and erode an otherwise welcoming and supportive atmosphere. Leadership practices that promote inclusion enable you to follow through on your promises and practice equity where it is most needed.

As a leader in diversity and inclusion, you'll need to develop an equity strategy that supports a rollout of improved policies and leadership practices throughout the rest of the team. Your equity strategy is a cornerstone piece in your inclusivity efforts. With a strong one, you can not only address policies that are currently recognized as discriminatory, but also put in place systems for evaluating and dealing with outdated policies in the future.

As the name implies, your equity strategy should be founded on the value of equity. This term is related to fairness and equality, but it differs in some important ways. Policies that promote equality correct for discrimination by treating everyone the same way. All employees or group members receive the same treatment and the same additional support, which helps them grow and thrive. This is a great first step, but it can sometimes fail to account for people's different levels of needs. For example, let's say you want to support your employees financially, and you've noticed that there's a difference in how much men and women are paid to do the same job. Following the rules of equality, you could resolve this issue by giving everyone the same raise. This succeeds in financially supporting the women who may have been less stable due to their lower paychecks, but it doesn't actually fix the inequality. At the end of the day, men are still being paid more than women.

This is where equity comes in. Rather than applying one flat adjustment across the board, equity involves assessing everyone's level of need and making changes accordingly. It means looking at which people and groups are facing the greatest struggles and giving them the support they need to succeed just as well as their peers. Using the following example of the pay gap, equity would lead you to address the situation in a different way. Rather than giving everyone the same raise, you could simply increase the salaries of female workers until they are being paid as much as men who do the same jobs. This eliminates the wage gap and ensures that everyone ends up on equal footing. It also keeps you from expending resources to help people who may not need the help, instead diverting these resources to where they can do the most good.

Your equity strategy, therefore, should target inequalities in policy and procedure. It should correct for these inequalities by trying to bring everyone up to the same level, offering assistance where it is most needed. Additionally, it should involve everyone in the group. Make sure managers, group leaders, and other administrators are all on the same page and working as part of the same team. To accomplish this, you'll need to focus on goal setting, outlining exactly what results you want to see and how you want to go about achieving these results. You'll also need to identify problem areas and work together with your staff to overhaul outdated practices. As everyone learns what is expected of them and gets on board with your efforts, you'll see significant change occurring throughout the entire group as part of a concentrated, coordinated effort.

Creating Measurable Goals for Staff

Diversity and inclusion efforts begin at the ground level, whether this is the staff of a company or the members of a club. Start by coming up with the goals you'd like to see your group achieve, then explain these goals to everyone so they understand exactly what's expected of them.

When creating effective goals, you'll want to keep a few basic principles in mind. First, make your goals specific. Understand exactly what you're trying to achieve, and identify methods for achieving it that you can pursue. A goal of "improve inclusivity" is an admirable one, but it's not especially specific, which can leave people uncertain as to how to go about achieving it. You'll want to break it down into smaller, more doable pieces like "hold one meeting about employee interaction and inclusivity policies each month," or "target and eliminate instances of harassment and bullying through improving policies about acceptable behavior." Once you have a specific direction to point yourself and others in, it becomes much easier to stick to your goals and see them through to the end.

Another key aspect of a good goal is making sure it's measurable. After all, if you can't measure your goal, how will you know when you've achieved it? Measurable goals come with the added bonus of allowing you to track your progress, which means you can see the positive results of every step you make toward your goal in real time. Decide on what benchmarks you'd be happy to see to consider your efforts a success. If you have an employee satisfaction survey, what percentage of positive responses would you like to see before you can call your new policies effective in promoting inclusivity? Should at least 80 or 90% of employees feel like they're in an inclusive environment, or will you not be satisfied until 100% of your team feels this way? Alternatively, you can measure your goals in terms of change. You might set a goal of a 50% increase in the number of employees who said they felt included. Whichever method you choose, make sure you have a way to tell how close you are to succeeding and how far you have to go.

Measurable goals also let you see when no progress is being made so you can revisit your strategy. This can be disheartening, but it's better than continuing to use strategies that simply don't yield the results you wanted. You'll be able to change your plans and recover much faster than if you had no idea how far you'd progressed.

Once you know what your goals are, work on informing every one of these goals and the methods you want to use to achieve them. Let your team members know that inclusivity is a priority for you and you expect them to join you in this venture. Lay out the expected behaviors they must follow, and explain any consequences that may occur if they refuse to comply with new policies and goals. Be very clear in your discussions, even if it means you have to be frank with people. It is better to be firm and explain your expectations than to have consequences that feel like they've come entirely out of the blue, catching people by surprise.

Above all else, make sure everyone cooperates and feels like a part of these new practices. Look for ways everyone can help, regardless of their role within the group. When everyone works together to achieve a goal, everyone gets to feel good about themselves when the goal is achieved. This also promotes unity within the organization, which gives team members a way to actively practice inclusion by working with a diverse group of people to accomplish a shared goal. This is exactly what diversity is all about, and it's the end goal you're trying to achieve with your policies.

Embedding in Performance Goals

In addition to the end goals you establish in your equality strategy, you should also have performance goals that act as markers along the path to success. These can be shorter, more easily accomplished steps that bring you closer to your goal, and they can be practiced by everyone.

Most importantly, embed these performance goals in the regular operations for your team. They should feel like natural extensions of what they're already doing and fit neatly into the pre-existing workflow. If people have to go out of their way to work toward inclusivity goals, they're more likely simply to shrug their shoulders and let someone else worry about it. When the task is already fairly similar to what they already do, it becomes no trouble at all to complete it alongside their typical responsibilities.

As people work toward their performance goals, you get another great opportunity to collect feedback from your team. Check in with them and see how they feel about the progress they've made so far. Ask if they feel like the current procedures are effective, or if there's something getting in the way of their ability to achieve the company-wide goals you've set. If there's an issue, adjust the performance goal or help them come up with an improved plan of attack that promises better results.

Working with HR and Management

Your management team should serve as your backup for inclusive leadership practices. They have leadership roles of their own on a smaller scale, which means they have a responsibility to act inclusively and with respect to cultural differences. Hold your management team to just as high a standard as you would hold yourself, as their actions can also help shape how the rest of the company feels about inclusion efforts and how effective these strategies are.

Your management team can oversee the implementation of specific aspects of your equity strategy. Their cooperation and understanding of your goals is integral to carrying out your goals. There's little point in reworking policies to eliminate discrimination in the hiring process if these new policies aren't followed by those in charge of the hiring process. Gathering all the information on appealing to different demographics in the world and building up your public image is useless if your marketing team's managers don't use this information. If your finance manager continues to pay people unequal salaries and perpetuate the pay gap, all the time you spent learning about this issue and developing a strategy to counteract it will become a wasted effort. Get your management team on board and be just as clear with your expectations for them as you would with your expectations for other team members.

One especially important position to include in your equity strategy is HR. They oversee the hiring process and deal with the allocation of employee benefits, which means there's a high potential for unconscious biases to interfere with company-wide equity. Additionally, if a team member experiences discrimination on an individual or systemic level, they're likely to bring their concerns directly to HR. If an HR manager is entirely unsympathetic to their problem, or if they don't fully understand how biases and prejudices can cause harm even when the harm wasn't intended, they might do or say the wrong thing. They could brush off concerns, downplay the issue, and fail to even inform you about the complaint. They may also perpetuate biases themselves, blaming the victim of the behavior. This does nothing to make the organization feel more inclusive, nor does it further your equity strategy. You might consider having special, additional training for people in HR positions since they'll need to deal with issues of race, gender, culture, sexual orientation, and religion more frequently than most employees.

The most important thing to keep in mind when developing inclusive leadership practices is that everyone should be involved in the effort. When everyone collaborates and you're all working toward the same goal, positive change is certain to result.

Chapter 15: Creating a Workplace Diversity and Inclusion Office

While every member of your team should be part of your equity strategy, and everyone should be aware of inclusivity efforts as a whole, you may also consider creating a special task force or group dedicated to overseeing diversity and inclusion policies. This is most common for companies with a decently large number of employees. You most likely have other important aspects of your job to attend to, so it helps to have a team who can address these issues in your absence. Since larger companies have so many employees, you might not have time to meet with everyone or double-check that your inclusion policies are being followed, but your diversity and inclusion office can certainly carry out these tasks.

This is not to say that you should be comfortable completely stepping away from being a leader who values inclusion. Your support of and involvement with this new team is still required, especially in the months after it is created and still finding its rhythm. In fact, your instruction will set the tone of how effective this new office is. By paying careful consideration to the best policies and directions the diversity and inclusion office can offer people in different positions throughout your company, you can create a self-sustaining system of checks and balances that educates employees and ensures there are no oversights throughout the entire company.

In order to establish and staff this office, you'll need to know exactly what its responsibilities are. In short, the diversity and inclusion office should function with the express goals of improving inclusivity, maintaining diversity, and analyzing the results of different policies in achieving these end goals. The office should be heavily involved in employee engagement, recruitment, retention of new hires, and talent management, and it should work collaboratively with the managers responsible for these tasks to ensure all diversity and inclusivity standards are being met. They may look at employee surveys and attitudes to reach a conclusion about whether or not certain policies are making the workplace more inclusive, or use data from other sources like measures of employee demographics. They can also suggest policy changes that could help remove opportunities for prejudice or harassment, which would later be reviewed and implemented by you. Perhaps most importantly, the office can provide you with feedback and advice regarding how positively people in the company feel about your inclusivity efforts so far and what you can do to improve their experience.

Workplace diversity and inclusivity offices target all main levels of the company's employees. They provide guidance to regular staff members, lead management groups in the right direction, and offer advice and support to you as the leader of your company.

Providing Staff Guidance

Staff guidance is the bread and butter of a diversity and inclusion team's efforts. An effective diversity and inclusion team will be able to examine interactions between staff members, identify problems, account for how biases and prejudices may be contributing to these problems, and suggest ways that these disputes and differences can be resolved. Inclusivity efforts that are supported by employees are typically far more effective than ones that are carried out without their input, so you'll want to be sure you're involving them in your team's efforts.

When working with the general staff of your company, you'll want to focus on education and outreach opportunities. Education can go a long way toward easing tensions. This means ensuring everyone who is part of the staff knows how inclusion efforts benefit them and how they apply to their daily tasks as mentioned earlier, but also encouraging staff members to learn more about each other's backgrounds and cultures. Discussions about race, religion, sexuality, and similar topics don't have to revolve exclusively around prejudices and injustices. They can also be celebrations of differences, and there are many ways to facilitate this.

You can start with a simple conversation where you encourage everyone to open up about themselves and speak honestly. You can also try more informal methods where learning occurs naturally, like hosting a multicultural potluck where everyone can showcase a meal that's important to their identity. It's also a good idea to eliminate any policies that restrict discussions about topics like religious and cultural practices, as these policies can unfairly impact people who are not part of the dominant culture and whose practices otherwise may not become normalized through discussion. While these policies can reduce the risk of disputes, they also make it more difficult to learn about each other. Provide accommodations for people to practice their religion as needed, such as a separate prayer room for those who are required to pray during the work day. The more everyone knows about each other, the easier it is to overcome boundaries between different groups and come together as a single, unified force. These are subtle ways of encouraging inclusivity, but they work just as, if not more, effectively as more obvious rules and regulations.

That being said, the staff of a company or other organization should also follow some basic rules that fall in line with diversity and inclusion efforts. Make it clear what harmful words and phrases are considered unacceptable in the workplace, as well as any behaviors that could be considered discriminatory, like giving the cold shoulder to certain groups of people or refusing to respect someone's boundaries. While these policies are necessary, they can sometimes feel restrictive. You can ease this feeling by giving employees more agency in diversity education, like offering optional classes that come heavily recommended but which don't force anyone to attend. Employees can sometimes look upon these methods more favorably, since they retain their sense of agency.

Discussions with staff members can be illuminating in regards to where the current diversity policies don't quite hit their marks. Managers have a general idea of how effective policies have been at combating barriers to inclusivity, but they might not have the same level of insight because they aren't part of the conversations taking place among staff members. Asking for feedback from staff members can show you weaknesses in these policies that you might not have identified otherwise.

Providing Management Guidance

Management teams can benefit from the guidance of a dedicated diversity and inclusivity department just like staff members can. They are responsible for overseeing employee interactions, so they should be made aware of some of the potential problems that can arise from issues with diversity and inclusivity. These include arguments between coworkers and an unwillingness to work together due to cultural differences and intolerance, which can significantly slow down productivity.

In these scenarios, the best guidance the diversity and inclusivity office can provide may be conflict management skills that involve considerations for diversity. If a dispute arises due to differences in religious beliefs, it's going to be incredibly hard to offer guidance if the mediator doesn't fully understand each person's perspective. They may find themselves siding with the person whose religious practices more closely mirror their own, whether this person was actually in the right or not. This kind of bias can cloud their judgment and interfere with their ability to come up with an appropriate compromise. When possible, managers should be instructed to pursue education about the different lifestyles and practices of their team members, and undergo training in order to hold their positions. If this education is not possible or it has not happened before a conflict takes place, you might consider having someone more knowledgeable about each side in the debate sit in and offer their opinions from a third-party perspective.

Management teams also need to be made aware of the ways in which bias can affect their own actions, which can have a harmful effect on employees. If the person in charge of performance reviews for a company is influenced by certain stereotypes, they may judge employees more harshly or more leniently depending on their identities. If the hiring manager has unconscious biases regarding who they believe is and isn't a good fit for the company, they may overlook excellent candidates in favor of ones that aren't nearly as capable. Education and bias training can go a long way toward solving these issues, helping managers be more cognizant of the prejudices and privileges that could be impacting their judgment.

Providing Leadership Support

The diversity and inclusion office is also responsible for providing guidance and support to you as the leader of your company or organization. As much as you might try to stay on top of issues and keep an eye on your own biases, there may be times when things slip through the cracks and you lack the outsider perspective necessary to recognize it. In these scenarios, it is very beneficial to have a diversity and inclusion office, as they can take note of these problems and bring them to your attention.

Perhaps the most important form of support that the office can offer you is suggestions about more inclusive policies. While you should always strive to be a leader in inclusivity efforts within your team, that doesn't mean you have the extensive knowledge or expertise needed to address every issue or conflict that can arise in a diverse group. Your point of view may prevent you from seeing how some policies are harmful or where some policies that attempt to improve inclusivity actually fall short of achieving their goals. Maybe a policy you tried to implement even risks having the opposite effect and increasing bias. Without a team pointing this out, you might not realize this until the damage has already been done.

With the support of a diversity and inclusion office, you can correct these mistakes, repeal bad policies that harm your employees, and focus your efforts on positive change once again. They can advise you on which policies you might consider replacing and what your next steps should be when addressing inequalities in the workplace.

Chapter 16: Additional Resources

This chapter contains additional resources you may find helpful to you as you continue to explore leadership in diversity and inclusion. You may reference them as you read through the book, or refer back to them to refresh your memory on topics that were previously covered.

Leadership Checklist

There are many factors you need to keep track of as a leader in diversity and inclusion. Multiple different goals may require your attention, and it can be hard to keep track of each of them if you don't have a good system for remembering everything you mean to accomplish. To make the process easier, you can use this leadership checklist, which includes a handy list of key topics and goals to address in your leadership methods as well as the reason why they are important.

This list is just an example of some of the many tasks you might set for yourself. It covers many of the topics discussed in earlier chapters of the book and can serve as a convenient review of the skills you have learned so far. It is not meant to limit you in any way, but instead to suggest some key points to focus on. You are welcome to expand it as you see fit to accommodate any additional goals you find to be important.

1. **Show your own support for diversity and inclusion first and foremost.** Maintain a positive attitude that rubs off on other members of the team. Be open about new policies, and try always to exhibit behaviors that emphasize inclusion. Work on recognizing and rejecting your own personal biases and prejudices so you can do the same for your company.

2. **Clearly define your expectations for diversity and inclusion.** Understand what you want to achieve and how you want to go about achieving it. Create a corporate strategy that aligns closely with your group or company's motto, values, and operational strategy. Define your goals, then break them down into smaller actionable steps. Once you've done so, communicate this information to the rest of the team so no one is blindsided by a future change in policy.

3. **Expand your hiring pool to support company diversity.** If you find you're lacking in diverse employees, the problem may be that you're just not attracting enough job candidates. Review your job requirements and listings. Are they too strict? Do they eliminate too many potential candidates right off the bat? Do they contain phrases that might function as red flags to

potential employees? Does your company have a bad reputation in regards to diversity that could be driving some people away? Adjusting for these issues gives you a more diverse pool of candidates to work with, which can help you find the best person for the job and avoid hiring people exclusively for diversity reasons.

4. **Look at diversity benchmarks across the company.** Diversity efforts don't end in the hiring stage. They don't even start here—they actually begin in the candidate pool. Examine and analyze data about the diversity of people applying for positions as well as the diversity of people who are accepted for those positions. See what you can do to improve diversity, whether that means changing hiring criteria or adjusting the methods you use for the interviewing process. Then, continue to trace diversity through the rest of the company. See how many people in minority groups remain with the company after a few months, or a few years, and identify any reasons for sharp drop-offs in employee retention. Consider diversity rates for people being offered promotions, and ensure there is diversity in your upper management that adequately reflects the population demographics of your regular employees.

5. **Designate a head of diversity.** Give your diversity task force a central leader who is responsible for the team's management. They will

be your point of contact for discussing the implementation of inclusion and equity strategies. Choose someone who has experience leading diverse teams and who genuinely wants to see people in the company learn and grow, creating a more inclusive place for all.

6. **Prioritize adding to the company culture rather than trying to define it.** Many people decide between job candidates by identifying who would be the best "fit" for the current company culture. While this can reduce the number of disagreements and help the organization feel more like a welcoming place to those allowed in, it also runs the risk of excluding people who don't happen to fit into the mold of the already existing culture. Rather than looking for those who would be a good fit, consider how much someone could contribute to the culture. Do they bring with them a perspective that was previously lacking? Are their skills an asset to the team? Over time, as diversity and inclusion efforts continue, people from very diverse backgrounds can grow to feel just as much like a supportive team as people who already share similarities.

7. **Always continue learning.** The goal of greater diversity sensitivity is to make everyone in the company more aware and respectful of each other's differences. You won't be able to improve your policies if you don't know much at all about cultures other than your own. For example, you

can't offer people the holidays off if you only know the Christian holidays and you have no idea which days are important to people of other faiths. Continue expanding your knowledge by any means available to you, whether through reading, finding information online, or simply by having more conversations with people of different backgrounds.

8. **Collaborate with people from your entire team.** Inclusion efforts need to involve everyone. You cannot have a workplace that is truly inclusive if there are still members of the group who resist these efforts. From executives, senior staff to administrative and operational staff, getting buy-in is crucial for your organization's culture to change and take root. Start with having leadership making a commitment to learning, promoting and influencing diversity and inclusive policies. Get everyone on board by explaining why these efforts matter and what you hope to achieve with them.

9. **Improve transparency throughout your organization.** Inequality can go unchecked simply because people don't have access to certain information. For example, differences in pay for employees might not get noticed if no one knows what anyone else is making. People may not realize that their coworkers are also struggling with a certain policy that unfairly targets them if they don't have the opportunity to talk to others

about it, or if they are discouraged from speaking about these things. Greater transparency means people can call out issues when they occur, and not when they become so significant that they are no longer possible to ignore.

10. **Accept that diversity and inclusion are continuous efforts.** If you're addressing these issues the right way, there won't be a clearly defined "end" to your efforts to make the workplace or organization more inclusive. There are always improvements to be made, and inclusion is an ongoing conversation. The goalposts for what makes a group inclusive may shift over the years, and this is perfectly natural. There will always be a need for diversity and inclusion efforts, which just emphasizes how important these skills are.

Privilege Checklist

Privileges can be tough to identify if you don't know what you're looking for. Since you are used to experiencing these privileges, they can slip completely under the radar and contribute significantly to inequalities within the workplace. To understand what privileges you and other members of your team may be enjoying which some may lack, refer to this privilege checklist.

- You don't spend much time thinking about your race and how it is perceived by others.

- You frequently see people of your race or ethnicity around in your neighborhood and in your workplace.

- Your success is typically attributed to your hard work and dedication rather than any affirmative action programs.

- Your failures and setbacks are attributed to either your own actions or bad luck rather than a stereotype about your race.

- People see you as an individual rather than a representative or spokesperson for other people of your race.

- You can afford to avoid conversations about race and privilege in your life, because they typically have very little bearing on you.

- You are not mocked or poked fun at because of your name or your hometown.

- You can easily request the day off for a holiday, or your company closes on these holidays so you automatically get the day off.

- You have never worried about your religious practices making people uncomfortable.

- You have never held yourself back from discussing your religion or displaying religious symbols.

- You have never been asked to remove a religious garment or symbol.

- You can visit new locations without having to worry about whether there are accessible entrances and exits for you.
- Your healthcare professional takes you seriously when you complain of feeling unwell.

- You have never been told you should not have children so as not to pass on a disability or other supposedly undesirable trait.

- You are free to express anger and take control of a situation without being called bossy or spoken about behind your back.

- You do not regularly worry about the risk of sexual harassment or assault, and you are comfortable walking alone in new places or at night.

- You can apply to jobs and be considered for promotions without being asked about your family.

- You know that police officers will believe you and take your side if you report a crime, and you feel safe around them.

- You can afford to cover your healthcare costs without too much issue, and you have never put off seeking treatment because you couldn't afford it.

- You can purchase new clothes you might need to appear professional at a job without breaking the bank.

- You have never worried about how you were going to pay for your next meal.

- You can afford to choose more expensive healthy meals when you want to eat them and junk food when you don't.

- You have never been denied access to a bathroom because of how you looked.

- Your gender is a listed option when filling out forms.

- You have never had to correct someone about your pronouns.

- People call you by the name you use to introduce yourself without question.

- You have never had to defend your existence to a total stranger.

- You have never had to "come out" to friends and family and risk rejection because of who you are or who you love.
- Your marriage to your significant other has always been recognized in the eyes of the law.

- You have never felt uncomfortable to talk about your partner in a public setting.

- You routinely see people like you in books, movies, and TV shows.

10 Diversity and Inclusion Questions to Use in an Organizational Survey

Ask staff to rate their opinions of the following statements on a scale from 1 to 10 (1 being strongly disagree and 10 being strongly agree).

1. This organization provides space for the free and open expression of ideas, opinions and beliefs.

2. Racial, ethnic, disabilities, sexual-orientation and gender-based jokes are not tolerated in this organization.

3. I often worry I do not have things in common with the colleagues on my team.

4. Management demonstrates a commitment to meeting the needs of employees with disabilities.

5. This organization has committed to take strict action against all forms of discrimination.

6. My manager handles diversity matters appropriately and demonstrates a commitment to diversity and inclusion.

7. I can voice a divergent opinion without fear of negative consequences.

8. In my organization, I can be successful as my authentic self.

9. Diversity & inclusion is one of this organization's stated values and/or priority areas.

10. Within the firm, everyone has access to equal employment opportunities regardless of their difference.

Conclusion

Leaderships skills for diverse teams that prioritize inclusivity aren't just useful tools to have. They are absolutely mandatory for being an effective leader. As workforces and the general population continually grows more diverse, these skills become even more important with every passing year. The greater the diversity on the team you manage, no matter what kind of team it is, the more important the lessons you have learned in this book will be.

While reading *Leadership in Diversity and Inclusion*, you have learned not just how to be a good leader, but also why. Throughout this book, we've taken a look at diversity trends and examined their impact on the ever-increasing need for better diversity and inclusivity policies. We've defined in detail what diversity and inclusion mean, understanding their differences and how they work together. We've looked at the difficulties you may face as a leader of a diverse team, but also all the incredible benefits that make it worthwhile. We've also examined common barriers to inclusivity, including microaggressions, unconscious biases, systemic racism and oppression, and privileges. Finally, we've opened the door to tough questions, embracing discomfort in an effort to carry out the best possible inclusivity strategies and policies for any group.

These are all critically important skills, and knowing them gives you a leg up as a leader. When you put these skills into practice, the returns will be well worth the effort. The morale of your team members who belong to minority groups will improve as they realize they have someone in their corner. The productivity of your team will increase as barriers break down and people work in synergy with each other. Everyone will get the opportunity to put their best foot forward and really excel in their position, unhindered by prejudices or biases. When you lead with diversity and inclusion in mind, you ensure your organization, group, or workplace is functioning at maximum efficiency.

As you put these skills into practice while leading your own team, remember what you've learned here. Diversity and inclusion are about so much more than just meeting quotas and complying with legal regulations. They are about showing your team members you respect them and that their health and safety matters to you. They are about learning and growing as a person as well as a leader. Ultimately, they are about improving the state of the world in whatever way you can, ensuring that everyone enjoys the benefits of becoming part of not just a workplace but a community, and finding where they truly belong.

References

Alberta Civil Liberties Research Centre. (n.d.). *The Myth of Reverse Racism.* http://www.aclrc.com/myth-of-reverse-racism

Bersin, J. (2019, Mar. 16). *Why diversity and inclusion has become a business priority.* http://joshbersin.com/2015/12/why-diversity-and-inclusion-will-be-a-top-priority-for-2016/

Bureau of Labor Statistics. (2019, Oct.). *Labor force characteristics by race and ethnicity, 2018.* https://www.bls.gov/opub/reports/race-and-ethnicity/2018/home.htm

Canadian Construction Association. (2019). *The value of diversity and inclusion in the Canadian construction industry.* https://www.cca-acc.com/wp-content/themes/cca/images/diversity/CCA_13413_Business_Case_EN.pdf

Catalyst. (2020, Oct. 20). *People of colour in Canada: Quick take.* https://www.catalyst.org/research/people-of-colour-in-canada/

Cohn, D. & Caumont, A. (2016, Mar. 31). *10 demographic trends shaping the U.S. and the world in 2016.* Pew Research Center.

https://www.pewresearch.org/fact-tank/2016/03/31/10-demographic-trends-that-are-shaping-the-u-s-and-the-world/

DeAngelis, T. (2009, Feb.). Unmasking 'racial microaggressions'. *American Psychological Association, 40*(2), 42. https://www.apa.org/monitor/2009/02/microaggression

DeWolf, M. (2017, Mar. 1). *12 stats about working women.* U.S. Department of Labor Blog. https://blog.dol.gov/2017/03/01/12-stats-about-working-women

Edwards, F., Lee, H., & Esposito, M. (2019, Aug. 20). Risk of being killed by police use of force in the United States by age, race-ethnicity, and sex. *Proceedings of the National Academy of Sciences of the United States of America, 116*(34), 16793-16798. https://doi.org/10.1073/pnas.1821204116

Elevate. (2015, Mar. 3). *Small ways leaders alienate female employees through gender-based criticism.* Forbes. https://www.forbes.com/sites/ellevate/2015/03/03/small-ways-leaders-alienate-female-employees-through-gender-biased-criticism/?sh=2ed35a66459e

Garr, S. S., Shellenback, K., & Scales, J. (2014, Aug.). Diversity and inclusion in Canada: The current state. Deloitte.

https://www2.deloitte.com/content/dam/De loitte/ca/Documents/human-capital/ca-en-human-capital-diversity-and-Inclusion-in-canada.pdf

Hcareers. (2020, Aug. 5). *Diversity and Hospitality Upper Management.* https://www.hcareers.com/article/employer-articles/survey-results-diversity-and-hospitality-upper-management

Hiranandani, V. (2012, Nov. 14). Diversity management in the Canadian workplace: Towards an antiracism approach. *Urban Studies Research.* https://doi.org/10.1155/2012/385806

LoBianco, M. (2016, Mar. 24). *Report: Aide says Nixon's war on drugs targeted blacks, hippies.* CNN. https://www.cnn.com/2016/03/23/politics/john-ehrlichman-richard-nixon-drug-war-blacks-hippie/index.html

McLaren, S. (2017, June 8). *How Airbnb is working to eliminate bias from its interview process.* Linkedin Talent Blog. https://business.linkedin.com/talent-solutions/blog/candidate-experience/2017/how-airbnb-is-working-to-eliminate-bias-from-its-interview-process

National Organization for the Reform of Marijuana Laws. (2020). *Racial disparity in marijuana arrests.* https://norml.org/marijuana/fact-sheets/racial-disparity-in-marijuana-arrests/

National Sexual Violence Resource Center. (2012). *False reporting.* https://www.nsvrc.org/sites/default/files/Publications_NSVRC_Overview_False-Reporting.pdf

Phillipe, M. Y., PhD. (2011, Aug. 31). *Diversity power in the corporate image.* Diversity Journal. https://diversityjournal.com/5695-diversity-power-in-the-corporate-image/

Van Ginkel, B. (2016, Oct.). *Business Development Bank of Canada: A Canadian success story in diversity and inclusion.* The Canadian Centre for Diversity and Inclusion.

Van Ginkel, B. (2017, Jan.). Blake, Cassels & Graydon LLP - A Canadian case study in diversity and inclusion. The Canadian Centre for Diversity and Inclusion.

Wong, K. (2020, Oct. 7). *Diversity and inclusion in the workplace: Benefits and challenges.* Achievers. https://www.achievers.com/blog/diversity-and-inclusion/